BOLD
FAITH

BOLD
FAITH

*A Closer Look at the Five Key Ideas
of Charismatic Christianity*

Ben Pugh

WIPF & STOCK · Eugene, Oregon

BOLD FAITH
A Closer Look at the Five Key Ideas of Charismatic Christianity

Copyright © 2017 Ben Pugh. All rights reserved. Except for brief quotations in critical publications or reviews, no part of this book may be reproduced in any manner without prior written permission from the publisher. Write: Permissions, Wipf and Stock Publishers, 199 W. 8th Ave., Suite 3, Eugene, OR 97401.

Wipf & Stock
An Imprint of Wipf and Stock Publishers
199 W. 8th Ave., Suite 3
Eugene, OR 97401

www.wipfandstock.com

PAPERBACK ISBN: 978-1-4982-8034-1
HARDCOVER ISBN: 978-1-4982-8036-5
EBOOK ISBN: 978-1-4982-8035-8

Cataloguing-in-Publication data:

Names: Pugh, Ben.

Title: Bold faith : a closer look at the five key ideas of charismatic Christianity/ by Ben Pugh.

Description: Eugene, OR: Wipf & Stock, 2017 | Includes bibliographical references and index.

Identifiers: ISBN 978-1-4982-8034-1 (paperback) | ISBN 978-1-4982-8036-5 (hardcover) | ISBN 978-1-4982-8035-8 (ebook)

Subjects: LCSH: Pentecostalism. | Holy Spirit.

Classification: BT121.2 P85 2017 (paperback) | BT121.2 (ebook)

Manufactured in the U.S.A.   03/03/17

Scripture taken from the New King James Version (NKJV). Copyright © 1979, 1980, 1982 by Thomas Nelson, Inc. Used by permission. All rights reserved.

Dedicated to Rev Dr. Keith Warrington whose leadership of the MA in Pentecostal and Charismatic Issues at Regents Theological College first introduced me to the fascinating idea that Pentecostalism could be studied academically by Pentecostals.

Contents

Acknowledgments • ix

Introduction • xi

1 Clearing the Ground:
   The Four Distinctives of Classical Pentecostalism • 1
2 Healing the Heart: The Inner Healing Movement • 24
   Excursus—The Shop Window: The Rise of Charismatic Worship • 38
3 Leading and Discipling: The Shepherding Controversy • 56
4 Praying Effectively: The Word of Faith Doctrine • 67
5 Conquering Evil Forces: Spiritual Warfare • 87
   Excursus—How do they Grow? Charismatic Evangelism • 106
6 Demonstrating a Living God: Signs and Wonders • 110
   Conclusion • 123

Bibliography • 127
Index • 143

Acknowledgments

As has increasingly been the case over the time that I have been part of the Faculty at Cliff College, the large and varied teaching load that I carry there brought this book into full form. I had conceived it about ten years ago but not until the academic year of 2014–15 did it get tested out in the classroom. In the wake of a one-off renewal event I had organized (a spiritual gifts workshop), I wanted a way of embedding an expression of renewal into regular college life as part of the degree program. The module, The Holy Spirit, Spiritual Gifts, and Pentecostalism was born. My desire was that the first ten minutes of each lecture (at least) would be given over to allowing the Holy Spirit to work among the students. We would not only be discussing him but experiencing him. I have taught the module twice now and credit goes very much to the students for the way they have engaged with it. One morning during the height of a movement of God's Spirit among the students (unrelated to my course, I hasten to add), I turned up to the classroom to find all the students huddled and praying fervently. I soon found myself brought into their hand-holding huddle praying for revival to come to the college. This book is, basically, most of the content of that course but without the teaching on the Holy Spirit and spiritual gifts, which I thought would need to be part of separate book projects.

Thank you, Cliff College, for being so open to the Spirit, and for giving me the chance to try out this course, and thank you to the two years' worth of Cliff College BA in Theology students who have chosen this module. You now have a home-grown text book!

Thank you also to Dr. Chris Spinks, my editor at Wipf & Stock.

Introduction

Trends and Taxonomies

As a former insider to the Charismatic networks in Great Britain, and more recently, as a "Classical" Pentecostal,[1] I have been both fascinated by, and at times alarmed at, the sheer creativity of the theology that is going on at a popular level within Charismatic circles. In fact, it has been something of a relief to reach, through my involvement with the Assemblies of God, the much calmer waters of a ninety-year-old denomination. I no longer need to contend with the tempestuous seas of high-octane Charismatic spirituality with all its triumphalism, faddishness, and restless discontent.

However, there are things that I miss about it. Charismatics are possessed of an indomitable sense of their own significance. Whatever God is doing in the churches happens with them first, or so it is believed. To be part of a Charismatic network is to find oneself within a group that has quite the most infectious sense of self-belief. I freely admit that, at its worst,

1. For the benefit of the reader who may be new to the subject, there is, within Pentecostal studies, quite a delectation for terminology. True connoisseurs of the subject are discernable by their constant questioning of the received taxonomy. Within Western Pentecostalism, detractors aside, there are generally understood to be three strands within Pentecostalism: the Classical Pentecostals—those whose denominations were founded in the early twentieth century; the Charismatic Renewalists—those who, in the 1960s–1970s entered into an experience of the Spirit and spiritual gifts within the historic non-Pentecostal denominations, *and have stayed in those denominations*; and, lastly, the Neo-Charismatics, New Churches, Apostolic Networks or Independent Charismatics (the terminology here is extremely fluid). These are those whose roots go into the Charismatic Renewal but who chose to *not* remain within their parent denomination. Distinctions continue to blur, however. Presently, I am in a city-wide apostolic network (the NG Church Network) that exists quite happily within the Assemblies of God, a Classical Pentecostal denomination.

Introduction

this self-belief makes it insular and conceited; but at its best it provides a heroic sense of corporate calling that rallies one's noblest energies. And it is this strong sense of corporate significance that feeds the kinds of theology that Charismatics tend to generate. As we will see, running through all these Charismatic theologies is a firm conviction that the power to control the universe resides with the believer. All of these theologies belie a restless and defiant refusal to allow other powers—whether physical or spiritual—to dominate, restrict or enslave the self. In almost every case, humanity's power over the universe is exercised through the power of speaking. In this way, the Word of Faith movement has now permeated every other theological distinctive. The cosmology of Tulsa's preachers is now virtually universal. Demonic powers are rebuked and bound in the name of Jesus; good powers are "loosed" in the confident assurance that, as a result of such pronouncements, something in the spiritual realm has changed, and no verification is needed.

I will trace the origins and development of five Charismatic innovations in chronological order of their appearance in history: Inner Healing, Shepherding, Word of Faith, Spiritual Warfare, and Signs and Wonders. Some of these beliefs have proven more durable than others, but in every case there can be found something definitive of the movement and indicative of the reasons for the movement's success. And it is specifically those theologies that are identifiably Charismatic, rather than Pentecostal, that I will be analyzing.

The division, of course, is problematic, and writers on the subject tend to group Charismatics and Pentecostals together under the heading "Pentecostalism."[2] However, not only is the twofold distinction necessary

---

2. Difficulties arise when trying to provide accurate figures for the growth of the movement. Global estimates range from 250 million adherents to 500 million adherents depending on who is included in the terminology: Anderson, *Introduction to Pentecostalism*, 11–12. Bergunder has recommended that we accept the fact that the terminology will never be definitive of such a diverse group and describes the phenomenon as a discursive network whose identity is always contingent: Begunder, "The Cultural Turn," 52–56. Robeck and Yong, while not quite that agnostic about terminology, fully embrace the immense diversity of "Pentecostalism": Robeck and Yong, "Global Pentecostalism," 1–10, and Vondey, *Pentecostalism*, 1–8. Despite this healthy recognition of diversity I have yet to come across a book that portrays Charismatic Christianity as a unique source of major theological innovation in its own right. It seems to be seen, and understandably perhaps, only as an off-shoot of Classical Pentecostalism, and I wonder if this is down to the fact that so many prominent scholars writing in the field have tended to be Classical Pentecostals themselves. Warrington, a Classical Pentecostal, is wise enough to set his parameters before providing his *Pentecostal Theology*, vii–ix.

Introduction

but a further distinction in terminology has often proved useful too, namely the distinction between "Charismatic Renewalists" and "NeoCharismatics."[3] This distinction applies mostly to Western countries and is a way of marking the transition to the House Church movement from the Charismatic Renewal movement. It was the point at which it became obvious that a significant mass of renewed Baptists, Methodists, Brethren, Anglicans, Episcopalians, and Pentecostals had now left their denominations and formed themselves into small groups that met in people's homes. In Great Britain, this realization roughly coincided with the Festival of Light in 1971.[4] It is within this third and most recent wave or grouping that most of the theological innovations discussed here have emerged.[5]

The provenance for the emergence of the beliefs I will be analyzing has been mostly North America, though with influences having entered in from a variety of places,[6] and with British Charismatics adding their own distinctive twists. These theologies have flourished mostly in the context of a heady new movement, loosed from denominational constraints. These historic denominations were understood to be inimical to the moving of the Spirit. It thus became a movement in search of new and flexible self-definitions, belief systems, and authority structures. Charismatic beliefs have thus emerged as a powerful concoction of immensely diverse denominational hangovers that were imported and re-invented by the first generation of "come-outers."[7] Indeed, every distinctive that will be analyzed here has its roots somewhere else, including some surprising non-Christian sources. The influence of Classical Pentecostalism is significant but not by any means definitive. Many Charismatics lack a clear theology of a baptism

---

3. Kay, while acknowledging the terminology of the three waves initiated by Barratt, prefers to use the term "Neo-Pentecostal" to describe all kinds of Charismatics: Kay, *Pentecostalism*, 11.

4. A book, with Cliff Richard on the front, marked the occasion: Capon, *And There Was Light: Story of the Nationwide Festival of Light*.

5. There is one place where the boundary between Charismatic Renewal and the Neocharismatics is blurred and that is with the doctrine of Inner Healing, which originated in the early days of the Charismatic Renewal but which today is being developed by independent Charismatic groups such as Bethel Church in Redding, California. However, so as not to be unduly tiresome about terminology, I have chosen to simply use the word "Charismatic" throughout this book, and what I intend by this term is mainly the Neocharismatics and not so much the Charismatic Renewalists.

6. E.g., Latin America (Juan Carlos Ortiz) and China (Watchman Nee).

7. The phrase used at the time to describe those who left their denominations to join one of the new independent groups.

Introduction

in the Holy Spirit, for instance, and are not at all precious about the Classical Pentecostal ideas of separation and subsequence and tongues as initial evidence.[8]

But why, now that the Charismatic Movement is so "old hat," do I want to study its belief systems in such depth? Well, Charismatic Christianity is still a form of Christianity that is growing explosively in the Global South and still thriving at the heart of the urban secular spaces of the West. It must surely have something to say, and a big part of this book's aims is to hear its prophetic voice. With the many volumes on all things Mission-Shaped, Missional, and Emerging that have been going to press in recent years there is, perhaps, the assumption that the Charismatic movement, if it can even be termed a "movement" any longer, does not have anything to add to the discussion. Yet even a cursory glance at the history of the movement reveals that it has, in many cases, already pioneered many of the solutions now being discussed.

It is my hope that in surveying the contours of these belief systems, we can emerge wiser as to what this prophetic group of people is trying to say to the rest of the Church as the Church finds itself pushed to the margins of society and in some parts suffering serious decline. If the essence of what Charismatic Christianity is saying can be captured, the Church and the world will be far the richer. The movement continues to be among the most daring, innovative, and controversial expressions of Christianity in the world today and a focused treatment of its distinctive theological responses to the situation in the West is overdue. It is a movement from which church practitioners can draw courage as they observe it attempting, however falteringly, to make bold and innovative responses to life on the margins.

Charismatics and Culture

A colleague of mine, Justin Thacker, once made a comment that has never left me. He defined Charismatic faith as a critique of late modernity. As I have reflected upon this I have found that my interest in Pentecostalism (broadly understood) and my interest in Western culture have begun to flow together.

---

8. Recent empirical research indicates that only 17 percent of British Charismatics believe that tongues are the initial evidence of baptism in the Spirit. Kay, "Apostolic Networks," 31.

Introduction

This latter interest began when I read the work of John Drane[9] at the end of the 1990s as I struggled to make sense of the cultural changes that had taken place over that decade. This was also the time when Brian McLaren[10] and the Emerging Church first emerged. Then, 9/11 happened, and the hopes many of us had that the postmodern shift might also open out into a post-secular shift, a shift to a more spiritually and religiously open attitude amongst people, were very soon dashed.

I noticed that, in many ways, the secular agenda was becoming far more forceful than ever, spurred on by the religious violence that it cited as its own justification. By the time we got to the end of the first decade of this century, chafing as so many of us were and are against the chains of amaranthine state regulation, I began to wonder just how postmodern we were. In fact, I more or less dropped the term and focused in my lectures on what I thought was a more worthwhile thing for Christians to address: post-Christendom. My belated reading of Stuart Murray[11] in 2012 was a paradigm shift and I began to delve into the literature of the ongoing missional church conversation. I found myself almost ready to cheer on the demise of Christendom in the belief that this was helpfully forcing the Church to recover its pre-Constantinian roots. It was as though life on the counter-cultural margins of a totally secular culture was to be greeted as empowerment rather than the disempowerment that it really was. In some ways, Pentecostals and Charismatics had already perfected ways of feeling powerful and anointed within our own parallel universe that never touched the real one. At our most insular, we had already learned how to identify with the primitive church of Acts and stay in that bubble.

Then, I came across critiques of Western culture, mostly from within the Radical Orthodoxy movement, which seemed quite agitated by this thing called the "secular." At first I thought it very passé that people could still be concerned about such a thing when in post-Christendom the Church is meant to have relinquished any claims to center stage within the culture. I equated secularity with post-Christendom and its triumph as roughly coinciding with post-Christendom's arrival in the latter half of the twentieth century.

John Milbank seems quite sure, however, that modernity and the secular agenda that serves it, arrived on the scene around the year 1300.

---

9. Especially his *Cultural Change and Biblical Faith*.
10. His *A New Kind of Christian* caused quite a stir at the time.
11. Murray, *Post-Christendom*.

Introduction

Catherine Pickstock, following William Cavanaugh, times the full triumph of the secular project from the end of the Wars of Religion in late Reformation Europe. Secularity benefited then, just as it does now, from the pretext afforded it by the religiously motivated violence of the time. What it conceals is the role it plays in causing religious extremism and violence precisely by pushing religion to the margins of public life. As Karen Armstrong has made clear,[12] it also hides the role that entirely secular political allegiances play in apparently religious struggles. Lastly, it hides the fact that it has its own religious agenda and is a religious faith commitment of sorts, not a neutral view from nowhere. Some of its most cherished ideals are either developed from Christian roots or else developed as a reaction against religion.[13]

It seems then that Christian thinkers are offering three alternatives for meeting the demands of the current situation. The first option is Postmodern Blending. This is inspired by the notion that by assimilating postmodern artistic styles and epistemologies and by using correlational practical theologies we will be able to communicate more effectively with the culture. The second option is pre-Constantinian Restoration. This is the post-Christendom option, drawing from the Anabaptist traditions and a little from Newbigin to create a response that is not married to the spirit of the age but is a way for the church to permanently change shape to make us ready to meet the demands not only of postmodernity but of whatever follows it. The third option is Pre-Modern Retrieval. This is what the Radical Orthodoxy movement advocates. RO's sources are Augustine, Aquinas, and even Plato, but they avoid the Bible for fear of allying themselves to any kind of fundamentalist biblicism. However, probably, it is precisely in funding the RO outlook not from pre-modern philosophy but from biblical theology that it could finally prove useful to some of us.[14] The London Institute for Contemporary Christianity has already begun to engage secularity using a biblically informed approach that they call whole-life-discipleship.[15]

---

12. In her chapter, "The Triumph of the Secular" of her *Fields of Blood*, 238–74.

13. "... all the most important governing assumptions of such theory [that is, secular social theory] are bound up with the modification or the rejection of orthodox Christian positions." Milbank, *Theology and Social Theory*, 1.

14. Smith, "What Hath Cambridge," 101. In a footnote he adds: "I am troubled by a lack of careful biblical exposition and scholarship amongst RO representatives. While proposing a theology that is radically founded on revelation, there seems to be a paucity of real biblical engagement."

15. Greene, *Great Divide*; Cotterell and Hudson, *Leading a Whole-Life Disciplemaking*

INTRODUCTION

This is discipleship that reclaims those parts of us that secular modernity wants to keep religion-free, namely, our everyday life outside of church. It is a biblically informed retrieval of what life was like before the invention of the secular. We will see that, in an often clumsy way and through trial-and-error, Charismatics have been boldly attempting to create theologies and practices that face in exactly this direction.[16]

I have come, then, to the conclusion that Charismatic theologies should be looked at using the resources of this third option: the pre-modern, pre-secular retrieval. Charismatics have not had a seat at the table of those that have been discussing these options but what they have done instead is to simply try out ways of openly challenging the secular worldview.

Charismatics have been relatively unconcerned about the implications of postmodernity. It does not affect them all that much. Both Pentecostals and Charismatics have always pursued such an experiential approach that they enjoy some degree of insulation from the shifting epistemological demands of the surrounding culture.[17] Those most threatened by the arrival of postmodernity (whether they know it or not) have been those most deeply wedded to the epistemologies of modernity, namely those of scholastic conservative evangelical bent: they seek to resist modernity but do so on modernity's rationalistic terms. As for the second option, there are points where the restorationist impulse of Charismatic faith finds common cause with advocates of a pre-Constantinian shift. Yet it is just as glaringly obvious that most of the theological innovations analyzed in this book are not even trying to look anything like the primitive Church. The closest to such an effort would be the Signs and Wonders movement. The Shepherding movement's restoration of apostles and prophets is also a clear gesture towards the Church's first century or so of existence. Mostly, though, it seems that the passions that drive these innovations are a militant desire to overcome the whole secular premise, the whole scientific materialist worldview, and to restore the right of Christians to owe primary allegiance

---

Church; Hudson, *Imagine Church*.

16. Granted Milbank himself would probably class Charismatic Christianity as among the "ideologically opposite contemporary forms that it assumes." Milbank, *Theology and Social Theory*, xv.

17. And their experiential approach critiques modernity in a way that finds common cause with RO: "Because of an emphasis on the role of experience, and in contrast to rationalistic Evangelical theology, Pentecostal theology is rooted in an affective epistemology—undoing just the kind of dualisms RO seeks to deconstruct." Smith, "What Hath Cambridge," 110.

Introduction

to the Lordship of Christ and be guided by his Spirit and his appointed leaderships rather than consigning our lives to the care of an overweening and bloated secular state.

Charismatic faith is a bold attempt to tackle secular modernity in a mood similar to RO but using different sources and with more pragmatic end points in mind. My method therefore, building on James K. A. Smith's article for Pentecostals, will be to look at each Charismatic theological innovation through a loosely RO lens. This, I hope, will deliver a result that is philosophically and culturally informed and able to see the best and the worst in the Charismatic response to secular modernity.

Whitsuntide 2016

1

Clearing the Ground

THE FOUR DISTINCTIVES OF CLASSICAL PENTECOSTALISM

This chapter is designed to help make my point that Charismatic theologies, which all have their own distinct drivers and genealogies, are worthy of entirely separate treatment to Classical Pentecostal distinctives. Later, I will even go so far as to indicate possible grounds for differentiating Charismatic faith from evangelicalism itself. For now, in order to be clear as to the aspects of Charismatic faith that I have left out, I want to briefly explain four distinctive doctrines that I view as central to Classical Pentecostalism and not so central to Charismatic faith but which are typically assumed to be central to both. All but one of these, as I mentioned earlier, predate the beginnings of Pentecostalism and were honed by the holiness movement. In chronological order of their emergence, these concepts were: Baptism in the Holy Spirit as separate and subsequent to conversion (late eighteenth century), Premillennialism (mid-nineteenth century), Healing in the Atonement (late nineteenth century), and speaking in tongues and other gifts as Initial Evidence of Baptism in the Holy Spirit (early twentieth century). Of course, these four distinctives did then bleed into the Charismatic movement, but Charismatics have tended to sit very loosely to all four of these and have come up with their own more compelling distinctives which are better suited to their more libertarian and this-worldly outlook.

I will describe the histories of each of these doctrines and sketch out to what extent they have had a role in Charismatic church life.

Baptism in the Holy Spirit

Phase One: The Second Blessing Becomes the Baptism in the Holy Spirit

Pentecostal spirituality is indebted to the Wesleyan foundation of a second blessing, the precursor of the concept of Baptism in the Spirit. The Wesleys, the holiness movement, the Welsh revival, and the Azusa Street revival, provide a chronology that is now well established.[1] It is important to note that John Wesley is not the originator of the Pentecostal doctrine of baptism in the Holy Spirit, however, and seems to have had reservations about John Fletcher's use of the phrase to denote the Second Blessing. In fact, Herbert McGonigle is of the conviction that both Wesley and Fletcher failed to make adequate links between their doctrine of a second blessing and the New Testament language of an empowering *superadditum*, and the New Testament always refers to the Spirit to describe this.[2] Nevertheless, it is Fletcher that made the following statement, "Adult perfect Christianity . . . is consequent upon the baptism of the Holy Ghost, administered by Christ Himself," and it is the teaching of Fletcher on the subject, rather than that of Wesley, that the holiness preachers followed.[3]

In the nineteenth century, it would be Phoebe Palmer that became influential in her adoption of baptism in the Spirit terminology. The language of Pentecost thus adopted was the shape of things to come for the holiness movement and beyond. Her doctrine of the Spirit based itself increasingly on Acts 2:17–21. This passage makes an explicit link between Spirit reception and the power as a "maidservant" to "prophesy." This shift from a Pauline to a Lukan pneumatology was becoming widespread in evangelicalism by mid-century thanks to Palmer.[4]

---

1. There have been pleas for the inclusion of other movements into the chronology of influential antecedents, principally: Randall, "Old Time Power"; Randall, "Days of Pentecostal Overflowing," in Bebbington, *The Gospel in the World*, 80–104, and Waldvogel, "Overcoming' Life," 7–17, yet contra Cartledge, "Early Pentecostal Theology," 117–30.
2. McGonigle, "Pneumatological Nomenclature," 71.
3. Wessels, "Sprit Baptism," 131.
4. McFadden, "Ironies of Pentecost," 63.

Clearing the Ground

Phase Two: The Concept is Extended to Include "Power for Service"

Meanwhile, Charles Finney, Asa Mahan and others at Oberlin—not Methodists but just as interested as Palmer was in the Second Blessing—were beginning to promulgate a new emphasis on the idea of Christian Perfection. Palmer, as we saw, was already beginning to gesture towards a Lukan emphasis. Finney and Mahan cemented this by insisting that the Baptism in the Holy Spirit had indeed a dual benefit: sanctification *and* empowerment for service. This baptism in the Holy Spirit could encompass the Pauline emphasis on sanctification as well as the Lukan emphasis on empowerment. This was combined with an approach to receiving the experience that had even more immediacy than Palmer's: the seeker must decide, he or she must choose God now, whether that be for the first time resulting in salvation or for the second time, resulting in sanctification.

By the time of the first Keswick Convention in 1875, many aspects of the Wesleyan message, especially its doctrine of Perfection had fallen on bad times in Britain, although it remained strong among the working classes.[5] Christian Perfection had not acquired the same critical mass of adherents in Britain as it had in America. Further, the middle classes who attended the Keswick Conventions were particularly keen to distance themselves from fanatical Perfectionist teaching.[6] Their slogan was "Holiness by faith in Jesus, not by effort of my own."[7] It was a holiness performed by the risen Christ Himself within the human heart in response to the believer's full surrender and identification with Christ in death and resurrection.[8] Keswick, likewise, taught the expectation of power as well as holiness. In

---

5. Bebbington, *Holiness in Nineteenth Century Britain*, 71.

6. See especially Elder Cumming, "What We Teach," in Stevenson (ed), *Keswick's Triumphant Voice*, 19–20. Having said this, Keswick was never dogmatic about its theologies and Bebbington sees Keswick as a synthesis of the Calvinistic and Wesleyan approaches: Bebbington, *Holiness in Nineteenth Century Britain*, 73.

7. Aldis, *Message of Keswick and its Meaning*, 39.

8. Most Keswick speakers spoke at considerable length about Christ being the one with whom believers are crucified, rendering them dead to sin, as well as the more traditional message of Christ crucified for us. The doctrine of co-crucifixion was also a very popular teaching in the early Pentecostal periodical *Confidence*, e.g., Boddy, "Divine Necrosis: Or the Deadness of the Lord Jesus," 3–7. Pastor Polman saw three steps to Pentecost: " (1) Justification through the Blood, (2) Sanctification by union with Him in Death and Burial, and (3) the Baptism of the Holy Spirit with this helpful sign as a divine encouragement." Polman, "Pentecostal Conference in Germany," 33.

addition, by slackening the emphasis on sanctification as a sudden crisis moment, they paved the way for the Pentecostals and Charismatics to later remove sanctification altogether from the whole Second Blessing idea, putting it back where the Reformed faith had it all along: as part of the Christian's life-long journey. A sudden influx of power for service, however, was easy to sustain from the book of Acts.

Phase Three: The Concept is Equated with a Worldwide End-Time Revival

The chapels of South Wales were influenced by the fiery evangelism of the Salvation Army, who had conducted highly successful campaigns in the Rhondda. The chapels were also influenced by the techniques of Moody and Sankey, by such Keswick speakers as F. B. Meyer, who himself tried to claim some credit for starting the Welsh revival of 1904, and by R. A. Torrey who visited Cardiff in 1902. Accordingly, Evan Roberts' theology was basically a Keswick-style, pneumatological spirituality of personal victory over sin and power for service:

> The baptism of the Holy Spirit is the essence of revival, for revival comes from knowledge of the Holy Spirit. . . . The primary condition of revival is therefore that believers should individually know the baptism of the Holy Spirit.[9]

Converts of the Welsh revival, known as "Children of the Revival" gathered in mission halls and many went on to become Pentecostal. Among them were George and Stephen Jeffreys. George Jeffreys went on to found the Elim Pentecostal churches. Evan Roberts himself resisted the Pentecostal movement, however, possibly because of the influence of Jessie Penn-Lewis with whom he spent most of his life between 1906 and 1926.[10]

Partly thanks to the travels of Jessie Penn-Lewis, news of the revival spread far and wide. Global press coverage of the meetings was unprecedented for Welsh revivals, despite services being held mostly in Welsh.[11] These fed hopes, which were already running high, of a final outpouring of the Spirit that would parallel the first Pentecost. The quality that would set this final outpouring apart from a run-of-the-mill revival would be the gift

---

9. Evan Roberts, cited in Whittaker, *Great Revivals*, 103.
10. Jones, *Instrument of Revival*, chapters 17–20.
11. Evans, *Welsh Revival of 1904*, 36.

of tongues, as at the very first Pentecost. After news broke of the Welsh Revival, lengthy prayer meetings were held in Los Angeles for revival to come to that city.[12] All across the city many churches and holiness groups were stirred to pray for Welsh Revival phenomena to be seen in Los Angeles. Finally, in 1906, Azusa Street would be accepted by some as the longed for outpouring.[13] There, finally, were occurrences of the Baptism of the Holy Spirit with the sign of tongues.

Two Blessings or Three?

Of some note at this point, with regards to the baptism in the Holy Spirit, is the presence within early Pentecostalism of two distinct takes on whether the baptism in the Spirit was in fact the second blessing or whether it ought now to be considered the third blessing. This depended upon whether you were part of a group that was willing to let go of the original Wesleyan idea of sanctification as a single crisis event or whether you continued to insist upon it, in which case you would end up with a Third Blessing as well as a Second.

The very earliest forms of Pentecostalism in America (especially if we include the Church of God in Christ, which began in 1897), were of the three-blessing type, later referred to as Holiness Pentecostal groups. They retained the original Wesleyan scheme of two nameable, dateable experiences, one of conversion, new birth, or justification by faith, and then a second, equally nameable and dateable, of entire sanctification. When these Wesleyans came into an experience of being filled with Spirit and speaking in tongues for the first time, they considered it a third blessing. This third blessing they called the baptism in the Holy Spirit, hence the Azusa Street congregants' claim was that they had been "saved, sanctified and filled with the Holy Ghost."[14] This third blessing was not for salvation or for sanctification but for the power to minister to others in spiritual gifts, healing, preaching and evangelism.

William Durham, who tried to take over the Azusa Street mission in 1911, was responsible for introducing a two-blessing version of

---

12. Synan, "Bartleman," xv–xvi.

13. Faupel helpfully summarizes all of this in his conclusion (*Everlasting Gospel*, 307–9).

14. Synan, *Century of the Holy Spirit*, 99. Synan is an expert on all things relating to Holiness Pentecostalism. See also his much earlier, *The Pentecostal-Holiness Tradition*.

Pentecostalism called "Finished Work" Pentecostalism. Durham reckoned that the sanctification of the believer was a work finished on the cross at Calvary and could therefore be claimed as part of the total salvation package, without the need for a second blessing. He continued to affirm that there was a need for a Second Blessing for power, however, and his understanding of the Baptism in the Spirit as an empowerment for service was the same as that of the Holiness Pentecostals. The Assemblies of God in America, the largest white Pentecostal denomination in the US, adopted this Finished Work, two-blessing version as standard, leaving the mostly black-led Holiness Pentecostals to continue to affirm a three-stage initiation process, which they still do today.

An obvious disadvantage in the two-stage model of AG, of course, is that sanctification, once so very important to early Pentecostalism, is effectively dropped altogether. Another issue is the racial segregation that resulted, which goes against the original inter-racial vision of Azusa Street's beginnings.[15]

In the UK, which became important to the formation of wider European Pentecostalism, there never was a three-blessing version of Pentecostalism. This was due in large measure to the Keswick background of most of the early leaders such as Alexander Boddy. Keswick never had been adamant on sanctification as a once-only event and favored a crisis followed by a process. The German, Dutch, and Swedish leaders shared this outlook. Hence, it was even easier for sanctification to be gradually dropped from European Pentecostal discourse. In spite of this, the first European Pentecostals laid great stress on the need for a prior cleansing with the blood of Jesus, which involved a lengthy and soul-searching confession of all known sin, before one could be a worthy recipient of so precious a gift as the "baptism in the Spirit with the sign of tongues."[16]

Charismatics did continue to emphasize the baptism in the Holy Spirit, indeed the defining origins of the Charismatic Renewal are that non-Pentecostals began to experience it. However, Charismatics seemed to very quickly become enamoured with a series of emphases (the ones that shape this book) which more or less eclipsed any particular fascination with the founding initiatory experience. In fact, as we shall see, the

---

15. Sadly, Assemblies of God in South Africa and Namibia also was not vocal in opposing apartheid: Horn, "Power and Empowerment," 7–24.

16. See Pugh, "Power in the Blood," 215–26 for detailed analysis of early British Pentecostal experiences of baptism in the Spirit preceded by "pleading the blood."

experience became so tied in with speaking in tongues for the first time that any expectation that the experience could be anything more profound than that was not always maintained.[17]

Premillennialism

John Nelson Darby, a disillusioned Anglican curate working in Ireland is the originator of dispensational Premillennialism. While at a conference in 1830, what was to become the central distinctive insight of this doctrine was given via a prophecy from a young woman from Edward Irving's church by the name of Margaret MacDonald. The prophecy was to the effect that the Church would be caught up, raptured by the Lord, before the Tribulation occurs. This provided Darby with the start of a way of mapping out the whole biblical salvation story into epochs, the very last one being the Millennial kingdom which would be set up by the Lord when he returns with his saints whom he snatched away just prior to the seven-year Tribulation. Darby, by the 1860s–1870s, was becoming well-known in America. Via James H. Brooks, Darby's ideas were introduced to C. I. Scofield whose reference Bible was published by the Oxford University Press in 1908.

Faupel tells the American story of how the postmillennial dreams among Perfectionists in the wake of the 1857–1859 revival were dashed by the American Civil War of 1861–1865, as well as the evils of urbanization, industrialization, and mass immigration.[18] The mood thus changed to a more pessimistic one, which proved receptive to premillennialism with its warnings of the world's impending judgment and the need for the Church to be ready for the return of the Bridegroom.

The British transition to Premillennialism among holiness groups, beginning at Keswick, mirrored this story in many respects. Among the causes of the increasingly premillennial outlook among all holiness groups in Britain towards the turn of the twentieth century, Glass highlights: "changing social conditions and the increasing antagonism that orthodox Christian theology generated in circles of social, religious and academic sophistication."[19]

---

17. Don Basham's very popular book was an example of an effort to bring some fairly thorough teaching on the subject: Basham, *Handbook on Holy Spirit Baptism*.

18. Faupel, *Everlasting Gospel*, passim.

19. Glass, "Eschatology," 133.

At any rate, by the time Pentecostalism emerges, the premillennial eschatological framework had become definitive. Premillennialism created the theological framework, informed the religious language, and supplied the spiritual atmosphere for everything the early Pentecostals believed. In his analysis of the early British Pentecostal periodical, *Confidence*, Cartledge points out:

> It is arguable that the expectation of the imminent return of Christ was the significant aspect to the theology of *Confidence* and that the other features must be seen as fitting into this overarching concern.[20]

The reoccurrence of the gifts of the Holy Spirit was the supreme sign that the Lord was coming soon: these were the long-promised days of the Latter Rain. Aside from the spiritual gifts, other miraculous occurrences, as in the days of the first outpouring—the Former Rain—could therefore be expected. Besides tongues, healing also took on this function as an eschatological sign.[21]

So the movement had a forward-looking and backwards-looking dimension: the Last Days were also days of apostolic restoration. Because these were the Last Days, an increase in anti-Christian satanic activity could also be anticipated, just as the Scriptures foretold:

> In these last days God is permitting His children to be tried. "Satan has asked for us to be sifted as wheat," not only in (sic) Satanic fury trying to overcome us and devour us, but *God* is proving us . . .[22]

Premillennialism was not optimistic about the state of the world.[23] So much was this the case that the blood of Christ, in the manner of the Exodus story, was needed over the door-posts and lintels of the human

---

20. Cartledge, "Early Pentecostal Theology," 126.

21. The campaign of George and Stephen Jeffreys in Swansea was hailed as an "Apostolic Revival" precisely because of the healings that were taking place, as well as the tongues, of course. George Jeffreys writes to Boddy, reporting, "The work here is deepening, and numerous conversions are taking place [a run-of-the-mill revival], and many have received the Baptism of the Holy Ghost with the Signs following. Praise the Lord! Some miraculous cases of healing have also taken place, and it is a real Apostolic Revival. . ." Boddy, "Apostolic Welsh Revival," 28.

22. Boddy, "Life out of Death," 110.

23. ". . . they expect things to go from bad to worse, and frankly tell me they have no hope of amelioration." Bebbington, "Advent Hope," 106, citing a postmillennial Methodist's comments on the mood of premillennialists.

heart. An especially interesting early Pentecostal article appears that shows a diagram of the heart (pictured as a house) with "the Blood" on its doorposts and lintels with, "Satan and his aerial hosts," written just above the house. These aerial hosts are unable to penetrate through the blood.[24] Such hosts as these were looking for opportunities to attack Christians that were earnestly seeking their own personal Pentecost.

There was a certain paradox about the early Pentecostal outlook: the constant despair of any answers to the downward trajectory of society on the one hand, necessitating the Lord's return and the end of the world, and the feverish expectation of a redemptive in-breaking of God in the here and now as a great revival sweeps the globe on the other. One reason why this contradiction was seemingly never harmonized would be the biblical literalism that was driving both interpretations of the end times. Because, as far as the Pentecostals were concerned, the Bible presented this twofold picture of both revival and deepening gloom without resolving it, so did the Pentecostals. Besides this, the dispensationalism of J. N. Darby that had been widely embraced by Pentecostals, had always affirmed that each new dispensation (including that of the End Times) begins with a show of miraculous power.[25]

Where Charismatics have found dispensational theology useful is as doctrinal support for their long infatuation with Christian Zionism. Already within the first few decades of classical Pentecostalism there was a fervent interest in in the land of Israel, especially following the start of the British Protectorate for the creation of a homeland for the Jews after World War I. Running alongside this was an increasing interest in a racial link with Israel: the belief that the Anglo-Saxon countries (Britain and America) were descended from the ten lost tribes of Israel. This fostered a physical sense of belonging to Israel and of being destined, in the millennial kingdom, to live there. This would be the final reuniting of Israel (the lost tribes) and Judah (the Jews). Many early Pentecostals were British-Israelists, for instance: John Alexander Dowie, Frank Sandford, Charles Parham, George Jeffreys, F. F. Bosworth, and John G. Lake.

This same kind of eschatologically-driven Zionism soon permeated the Charismatic movement. As early as the creation of the New Order of

---

24. Anon., "Faith in His Blood," 188.

25. See Smith, "Signs of the Times," in Brewster, *Pentecostal Doctrine*, 381–90 for something approaching a definitive outline of the Elim understanding of dispensationalism current at that time.

the Latter Rain, which came out of the Latter Rain movement in Canada from 1948, there emerged the teaching that two of the three Jewish feasts have been fulfilled, leaving only Tabernacles.[26] Much later on, but in line with this linking together of natural Israel with the spiritual Church, Derek Prince insisted that it was no coincidence that the outbreak of classical Pentecostalism at the turn of the twentieth century was at the same time that Theodore Herzl was starting the Jewish Zionist movement, or that the declaration of the State of Israel in 1948 was the same time that the great healing revival broke out, or that the miraculous six day war happened at the same time that Catholic Charismatic Renewal started.[27]

Just at the end of the sixties, large numbers of disaffected young Jews in America began to join the Jesus People and became Messianic. There remains a strong Messianic (and mostly Charismatic) Jewish section of the American Church. Such churches also attract Gentile Christians in large numbers. Not surprisingly, this influx of Jews into Charismatic Christianity bolstered already strong tendencies to identify with Israel and the Jewish people.[28] Besides Jewish-style worship songs in the seventies and eighties, Reuven Doron's *One New Man* of 1993 (and Sid Roth's *The Incomplete Church: Unifying God's Children* of 2007, and the *One New Man Bible* of 2011) further cemented this eschatologically-flavored desire for a reunification of Christianity with Judaism.

Leading figures in the Charismatic Christian Zionist movement today include John Hagee, leader of Christians United for Israel, as well as Pat Robertson. Hagee, however, denies any connection to his eschatological beliefs:

> Our support for Israel has absolutely nothing to do with end-times prophecy. It has absolutely nothing to do with eschatology. We support Israel because we feel that Israel is in greater danger than at any time in statehood.[29]

One of the prime motives in Hagee's case, as in many others, is what has been termed a "calculus of blessing," a similar principle as the sowing and reaping law that is often declared in Word of Faith settings as a motive to give financially. The call, implied by Gen 12:3, to bless Israel and so be

---

26. Warnock, *Feast of Tabernacles*.
27. Williams, "Pentecostalization of Christian Zionism," 182.
28. Ibid., 186.
29. Frykholm, "Calculated Blessings," 36.

blessed, operates in a similar way.³⁰ The dread of being cursed by God if the Jews are not blessed by a particular nation (and Hagee is clearly thinking at a national level more than a personal level) is what gives rise to the mildly censorious tone that Christian Zionists can sometimes take:

> For some time, churches across America have observed a unique group of Christians coming to worship services. They wear Jewish prayer shawls and Star of David jewelry, greet fellow congregants by saying 'Shalom,' and stop people after the service, a ram's horn tucked under one arm, to explain why every believer needs to go to Israel.³¹

Christian Zionism has, in fact, a tendency to instrumentalize Israel. There is what seems to be a strong philosemitism to the point where everyone else is guilty of antisemitism unless proven otherwise. Yet, the actions taken to support the Jews can include such things as Ulf Eckman raising money to help as many as 20,000 Eastern European Jews return to their homeland. Why? Because then biblical prophecy will be fulfilled. Relative to others, Eckman refrains from "large-scale end-time scenarios,"³² in his books. Other writers are not so restrained and include such things as Armageddon, which will result in one third of Israel being annihilated: all in the service of Christian eschatological verification.

Significantly, Hagee does not wish or require the Jews to accept Christ: they already are God's chosen people and will accept Christ at the Second Coming.³³ This was also held by John Alexander Dowie: God knew that the Jews would not accept Jesus and has purposed that they will accept him at his Second Coming.³⁴

---

30. Ibid. This belief probably has its origins within the comments on that verse within the Scofield Reference Bible. See this badly made but, in places quite plausible clip from a former adherent, Charles Carlson: "The Roots of Christian Zionism: How Scofield Sowed Seeds of Apostasy." https://www.youtube.com/watch?v=IO6VpMYAVms. His analysis of Gen 12:3 in successive editions of the Scofield Bible starts at 32:14.

31. Williams, "Pentecostalization of Christian Zionism," 183, quoting Stearns, "Why Israel Matters," 41.

32. Steiner, "War and Peace Theology," 47.

33. Frykholm, "Calculated Blessings," 36.

34. Williams, "Pentecostalization of Christian Zionism," 177.

Healing in the Atonement[35]

A Pentecostal concept with a nineteenth-century prehistory almost as long as that of the Baptism in the Holy Spirit and Premillennialism is the doctrine that physical healing is available by faith on the basis of the atonement, in exactly the same way and to the same degree as the forgiveness of sins. The only logical reason to fail to be healed in response to prayer ministry, therefore, was a defective faith either in the minister or in the recipient of the ministry, since Christ's atoning work cannot be deficient.[36]

The first major work to appear that promoted this view was that of A. J. Gordon, *The Ministry of Healing*, first published in 1882,[37] the title of which coined the now commonly used phrase, "ministry of healing."[38] The ideas behind this book, however, are traceable to the teachings of holiness preachers William Boardman and Carrie Judd Montgomery, which first emerged around the year 1880.[39] It does not seem possible to trace healing in the atonement back any further than 1880. Although the origin

---

35. This is an adaptation from Pugh, *Atonement Theories: A Way Through the Maze*, 97–105, used by permission of Wipf and Stock Publishers. See *Atonement Theories*, 99–105 for a detailed evaluation of the doctrine.

36. Interestingly, according to research carried out among British Pentecostal ministers in 1999, while 86 percent of those surveyed agreed with the statement, "Physical healing is provided by Christ's atonement," 60 percent disagreed (some strongly) with the statement, "Divine healing will always occur if a person's faith is great enough." Kay, "Approaches to Healing," 120–21.

37. Available in Graf, *Healing: The Three Great Healing Classics*.

38. Wilkinson, "Physical Healing and the Atonement," 151, n. 4.

39. Petts, "Healing and the Atonement," 12–13. See also Dayton, *Theological Roots of Pentecostalism*, 115–41. Synan traces the origins to a book by Otto Stockmayer: *Sickness and the Gospel*, of 1878, though he agrees that A. J. Gordon was the one who "elevated divine healing to the level of the atonement." Synan, "Healer in the House?" 191. Besides those of Petts, Dayton, Wilkinson and Synan, other academically credible treatments of the subject of healing in the atonement (some in favor of it and some not) include: McCrossan, *Bodily Healing and the Atonement* (1930); Unger, "Divine Healing," (1971); Hubbard, *Isaiah 53: Is There Healing in the Atonement?* (1972); Moo, "Divine Healing in the Health and Wealth Gospel" (1988); Bokovay, "The Relationship of Physical Healing to the Atonement," (1991); Niehaus, "Old Testament Foundations: Signs and Wonders in Prophetic Ministry and the Substitutionary Atonement of Is. 53," in Grieg and Springer, *The Kingdom and the Power* (1995), 48–50; Mayhue, "For What did Christ Atone in Isa 53:4–5?" (1995); Seet, "The Doctrine of Healing in the Atonement" (1996); Reichenbach, "By His Stripes We Are Healed" (1998); Menzies, "Healing in the Atonement," in Menzies, and Menzies, *Spirit and Power* (2000), 160–168. Interest in the subject now appears to be waning.

of the Faith Cure movement (of which Boardman, Montgomery and Gordon were a part) is traceable to Charles Cullis whose ministry began in 1865, it is clear that, as late as 1879, Cullis was making no attempt to give a theological rationale for divine healing.[40] The doctrine emerges gradually through various books and publications before reaching its fully developed form in A. J. Gordon. It seems likely that the original spark was provided by William Boardman noticing the way Ps 103:3 juxtaposes physical healing with forgiveness.[41]

One of the aims of the early writers, all of whom were engaged in mass evangelism in America, was to elevate the status of healing ministry by placing it at the center of Christian theology, namely, at the cross.[42] Offering not only the opportunity to be born again but also to be physically healed was already drawing large crowds but to link the offer of healing with the center-piece of the Christian faith was, in an age of virulent cessationism, to give healing ministries badly needed credibility.

Here is A. J. Gordon:

> He who entered into mysterious sympathy with our pain—which is the fruit of sin—also put Himself underneath our pain, which is the penalty of sin. In other words the passage [Isa. 53:4–5] seems to teach that Christ endured vicariously our diseases, as well as our iniquities.[43]

And A. B. Simpson:

> Therefore as he hath borne our sins, Jesus Christ has also borne away, and carried off our sicknesses; yea, and even our pains, so that abiding in Him, we may be fully delivered from both sicknesses and pain. Thus by His stripes we are healed. Blessed and glorious Burden-Bearer.[44]

The Pentecostal Carrie Judd Montgomery adds: "If we trust fully to His finished work, sickness shall not be able to hold us captive, for Christ 'himself took our infirmities, and bare our sicknesses.'"[45] And, anticipating

---

40. Wilkinson, "Physical Healing and the Atonement," 151, referring to Cullis' booklet of 1879 entitled, *Faith Cures, or Answers to Prayer in the Healing of the Sick*.

41. Petts, "Healing and the Atonement," 12, citing Mary Boardman, *Life and Labors*, 232.

42. Synan, "Healer in the House?" 192.

43. Gordon, *Ministry of Healing*, 16–17.

44. Simpson, *Gospel of Healing*, 17.

45. Judd Montgomery, *The Prayer of Faith*, 58.

Derek Prince's "wonderful exchange" teaching, F. F. Bosworth asserts, "Sin and sickness have passed from me to Calvary—salvation and health have passed from Calvary to me."[46]

The main biblical source for the doctrine is Isa 53:4–5 and the New Testament citations of it in Matt 8:17 and 1 Peter 2:24. If translated literally, Isa 53:4 would indeed yield phrases such as, "our sicknesses," and "our pains" to describe what the servant bore. For Bosworth, the meaning is clear: "This prophecy, therefore, gives the same substitutionary and expiatory character to Christ's connection with sickness that is everywhere given to His assumption of our sins."[47]

One especially notable Charismatic exponent of healing in the atonement was Derek Prince (1915–2003). Part of his *Keys to Successful Living* series included such teachings as "The Exchange at the Cross,"[48] recorded in 1989 and "The Cross in My Life,"[49] recorded at Kensington Temple in 1992. Such talks then appeared as a small book in 1995, *The Divine Exchange*,[50] and were finally collated into a larger work, *Atonement*, in 2000.[51] Throughout these, the same essential set of teachings is repeated. It is summed up in the form of nine exchanges, the second of which was: "Jesus was wounded that we might be healed."[52]

All of this teaching had its root in an encounter with two Christians in the back of a car during World War II in Suez. They offered prayer for his physical healing from a chronic skin condition. One of them spoke in tongues and delivered an interpretation that Prince describes as being in exquisite "Elizabethan English": "Consider the work of Calvary: a perfect

---

46. Bosworth, *Christ the Healer*, 26.
47. Ibid., 27.
48. Prince, "Redemption: Plan and Fulfilment: The Exchange at the Cross."
49. Prince, "Kensington Temple Sep 1992. The Cross in My Life."
50. Prince, *The Divine Exchange: The Sacrificial Death of Jesus Christ on the Cross*.
51. Prince, *Atonement: Your Appointment with God*.
52. Ibid., 37. The others were: "1. Jesus was punished that we might be forgiven . . . 3. Jesus was made sin with our sinfulness that we might be made righteous with His righteousness. 4. Jesus died our death that we might share His life. 5. Jesus was made a curse that we might receive the blessing. 6. Jesus endured our poverty that we might share His abundance. 7. Jesus bore our shame that we might share His glory. 8. Jesus endured our rejection that we might enjoy His acceptance. 9. Our old man died in Jesus that the new man might live in us."

work, perfect in every respect, perfect in every aspect."[53] Without having received healing at that point, these words soon led to a discovery:

> The essence of my discovery was this: On the cross a divinely ordained exchange was enacted in which all the evil due to our sinfulness came on Jesus, that in return all the good due to His spotless righteousness might be made available to us.[54]

When he comes to physical healing as provided for in the atonement, he takes a familiar assured line: "It is finished! As far as God is concerned, healing has already been obtained. We are healed,"[55] and he is certain that, "If you do not believe that God has provided healing in the first place . . . you are not likely to appropriate it."[56] However, because his doctrine of healing in the atonement has been made to fit within a broader metanarrative of exchange, its logic is undergirded and its fault lines become less visible. In this way, the problematic elements are not removed; they simply become smaller. Prince locates healing as only one of nine great benefits afforded by the exchange at the cross, all of which operate in the same way and in response to faith.

John Wimber never emphasized healing in the atonement as the theology behind his ministry, but preferred the "already-but-not-yet" kingdom theology of George Eldon Ladd. When he does touch upon the atonement in relation to healing he seems to deploy an atonement theology resembling recapitulation:

> Everything the devil introduced to men and women was undone by Jesus at the cross, which of course includes sickness. Jesus, the new Adam, came to restore us, to reproduce his new nature in us—which touches every part of our beings.[57]

He then goes on to integrate atonement with his kingdom theology:

> Because our sins are forgiven at the cross and our future bodily resurrections are assured through Christ's resurrection, the Holy Spirit can and does break into this age with signs and assurances of the fullness of the kingdom of God yet to come.[58]

53. Ibid., 24–25.
54. Ibid., 8.
55. Ibid., 49.
56. Ibid., 45.
57. Wimber and Springer, *Power Healing*, 165.
58. Ibid., 167.

Tongues (and Other Gifts) as Initial Evidence

The earliest Pentecostals held fervently to the premillennial expectation of a final deluge of the Spirit just prior to Christ's return that would include a renewal of the spiritual gifts.[59] In addition to their understanding of baptism in the Spirit as separable and subsequent[60] to conversion and as primarily an enduement of power for service, the Pentecostals also held that the initial evidence of this event would normally be a manifestation of the gift of tongues. In fact, the only unique thing about Pentecostal doctrine was the confirming sign of tongues. It became written into the founding documents of Pentecostal denominations. The following extract from the American Assemblies of God's *Fundamental Truths* in its description of separation and subsequence is an example:

> All believers are entitled to and should ardently expect and earnestly seek the promise of the Father, the baptism in the Holy Ghost and fire, according to the command of our Lord Jesus Christ. This was the normal experience of all in the early Christian Church. With it comes the enduement of power for life and service, the bestowment of the gifts and their uses in the work of the ministry (Luke 24:49; Acts 1:4, 8; 1 Corinthians 12:1–3). This experience is distinct from and subsequent to the experience of the new birth (Acts 8:12–17; 10:44–46; 11:14–16; 15:7–9).[61]

This theological framework, though potentially restrictive, provided a means for each generation of Pentecostals to pass on to the next one the same expectation of an experience that must be sought in addition to conversion. This framework enabled Pentecostalism to retain its original impetus through successive generations where other comparable movements might fizzle out within a generation.

In wider evangelical circles, a punctiliar, crisis conversion was encouraged. In Pentecostal teaching, not only a crisis conversion but also a subsequent crisis encounter with the Spirit was expected. Some say that the expectation of a crisis conversion sets the bar too high as it is. The expectation of a second crisis event arguably sets the bar higher still leading either

---

59. See Dayton, *Theological Roots of Pentecostalism*, 143–71.

60. On separation and subsequence see Robert and William Menzies's defense: *Spirit and Power*, as well as Gordon Fee's rejection of it: *Gospel and Spirit*, 105–19.

61. Cited and discussed at length in ibid.

to the perception of two classes of Christian[62] or a failure in reality to meet either of these expectations.

The point of the initial evidence was that there had to be some concrete supernatural evidence that you had received the baptism in the Spirit. Bear in mind that this was at the height of modernist scientism. Pentecostals were answering the culture's shrill demands for evidence just as much as they were seeking evidence for their own faith. The quietism of Keswick, therefore, would not do. Palmer's altar theology would not do. The Joel prophecy about the outpouring of the Spirit as it found fulfilment on the Day of Pentecost encouraged the first Pentecostals to look for more than simply taking it "by faith."

First and foremost among these evidences would be speaking in tongues. If that was the way it happened at the time of the "former rain" (in the language of Joel's prophecy), then this must be how the "latter rain" would look too. We were to look for a new Pentecost.

Charles Parham felt he had found this initial evidence with the help of his Bible school students at Topeka during an all-night prayer meeting in 1900–1901. They identified five Spirit baptisms in the book of Acts, three of which gave tongues as the confirming sign:

1. The day of Pentecost. Acts 2:1–4. Tongues.

2. Samaria. Acts 8:14–19. No tongues.

3. Ananias praying for Saul. Acts 9:17–18. No tongues.

4. Cornelius' household. Acts 10:44–47. Tongues.

5. Ephesus. Acts 19:1–6. Tongues.

Parham queried with his students this absence of tongues from two of the accounts. In response, the students explained the absence of tongues from Saul's (Paul's) Spirit baptism by reference to his clear statement in 1 Cor 14:18: "I thank my God I speak in tongues more than you all." The students proposed that he received this gift when Ananias prayed over him. Tenuous perhaps, but their argument about the Samaritan believers is stronger and, coincidentally, often used by scholars today: whatever happened there, it is clear that something happened, otherwise why would Simon Magus have offered money to get the power to impart this magical, supernatural thing that he saw. Parham's students reasoned:

---

62. Smail, "Cross and the Spirit," in Smail, Walker, and Wright, *Charismatic Renewal*, 57. Also Dunn, *Baptism in the Holy Spirit*.

> What could he have seen that was so special? Not miracles, or healings, because he'd already seen Christians doing these things. . . . No, when Peter and John arrived and Samaritan Christians received the Holy Ghost, Simon saw something new, something different.[63]

Interestingly, Parham himself did not receive the gift of tongues until three days later on 3 January 1901. Seymour and Boddy were, likewise, relatively late in receiving the very thing they ardently preached.

The gifts of the Spirit have retained a place of importance among charismatics. There have been principally two developments. The first was that the gift of tongues moved from being the initial evidence that baptism in the Spirit had been received to becoming equated with the baptism in the Spirit itself. There was increasingly the sense that speaking in tongues for the first time *was* the baptism in the Spirit. Gone were the lengthy tarrying meetings of the early Pentecostals. Gone was the soul-searching and the cleansing of the blood. To illustrate this, here are some testimonies of baptism in the Holy Spirit experiences, three from early Pentecostalism dating to the years 1908 and 1909, and the other rather more matter-of-fact experience of Charismatic pioneer Dennis Bennett, dating to 1960.

> After 14 days' fasting and longing to receive the Holy Ghost, I asked the Lord one evening so to purge me that I might not continue in sin. I asked the Lord to make it a reality, and a wonderful joy and purity streamed through my body and lit up all things around me.[64]

Kenyon, likewise, reports a ". . . willingness to give up things that hindered from finding full satisfaction in Christ, the Holy Spirit then took fuller possession."[65] She beautifully sums the results of her baptism in the Spirit as . . .

> . . . not a goal . . . but an entrance gate into a fullness of life in Christ. A life of wondrous possibilities lived on a plane few have

---

63. These events are reported in a highly engaging way in a popular book written during the Charismatic Renewal: John Sherrill, *They Speak with Other Tongues*, 30–42. This extract is from page 35. He is not declaring his sources and probably not reproducing the actual dialogue but providing an interesting dramatized account.

64. Anon., "Conference in Germany," 6.

65. Kenyon, "Testimony from Bracknell," 9

an adequate conception of, a life growing in fullness, a life of communion with the Eternal God through the Holy Spirit.[66]

A man writing in from Pretoria had already received "sanctification by the power of the blood" and was lying on a sofa reading a travel book:

> . . .when the power of God came upon me, and I was put upon the floor face down. I was two hours down there before I could let Jesus have His way. Praise Jesus, He did have His way, and I praised Him in the tongue He gave me.[67]

Dennis Bennett was Vicar of St Mark's Episcopalian Church, Van Nuys, California from 1953 until 1960 when the controversy generated by his public admission to having spoken in tongues led to his resignation. He tells how he receives the baptism in the Holy Spirit thusly:

> "What do I do?" I asked them again.
> "Ask Jesus to baptize you in the Holy Spirit," said John. "We'll pray with you, and you just pray and praise the Lord."
> I said: "Now remember, I want this nearness to God you have, that's all; I'm not interested in speaking with tongues!"
> "Well" they said, "all we can tell you about this is that it came with the package!"
> John came across the room and laid his hands first on my head, and then on my friend's. He began to pray, very quietly, and I recognized the same thing as when Bud had prayed with me a few days before: he was speaking a language I did not understand, and speaking it very fluently. He wasn't a bit "worked up" about it, either. Then he prayed in English, asking Jesus to baptize me in the Holy Spirit.
> I began to pray, as he told me, and I prayed very quietly, too. I was not about to get even a little bit excited! I was simply following instructions. I suppose I must have prayed out loud for about twenty minutes—at least it seemed to be a long time—and was just about to give up when a very strange thing happened. My tongue tripped, just as it might when you are trying to recite a tongue twister, and I began to speak in a new language!
> Right away I recognized several things: first, it wasn't some kind of psychological trick or compulsion. There was nothing compulsive about it. I was allowing these words to come to my lips and was speaking them out of my own volition, without in any

---

66. Ibid.
67. Armstrong, "South Africa," 20.

way being forced to do it. I wasn't "carried away" in any sense of the word, but was fully in possession of my wits and my willpower. I spoke the new language because it was interesting to speak a language I had never learned, even though I didn't know what I was saying. I had taken quite a while to learn a small amount of German and French, but here was a language "for free." Secondly, it was a real language, not some kind of "baby talk." It had grammar and syntax; it had inflection and expression—and it was rather beautiful. I went on allowing these words to come to my lips for about five minutes, then said to my friends:

"Well! That must be what you mean by 'speaking in tongues'—but what is it all about? I don't feel anything!"

They said joyfully:

"Praise the Lord!"[68]

A second new development was that the Charismatics displayed a much greater attachment to prophecy than did the early Pentecostals. In fact, it is difficult to over-state the unbounded enthusiasm Charismatics have shown towards the idea of being able to hear from God in a very immediate way.[69] It was an enthusiasm fed by the paperbacks of Bishop David Pytches,[70] reports of the remarkable but controversial Kansas City Prophets,[71] the more moderate voice of Morning Star Ministries founded by Rick and Julie Joyner,[72] and the somewhat critical voices of Clifford and Monica Hill.[73]

As a young Christian I can still remember how few things thrilled me more than the thought of being a prophet. And herein lies the key difference. Charismatics are attracted to the "office" or function of prophet or seer and view prophesying as a rung on the ladder, perhaps, towards the attainment of that status. For the Pentecostals, to be able to use the gifts at all was a big enough thrill and, on Robert Mapes Anderson's reckoning, this

---

68. Bennett's experiences are all recorded in his autobiographical *Nine O'Clock in the Morning*.

69. Joseph Hedgecock has founded an entire ministry around this: http://www.solm.org/INT/

70. Pytches, *Does God Speak Today?*; Pytches, *Some Said it Thundered*.

71. Maudlin, "Seers in the Heartland."

72. Founded in 1985.

73. Hill and Hill, *And They Shall Prophesy!* and the magazine *Prophecy Today*, which began in March 1985 but since 2015 has been entirely online: http://www.prophecytoday.uk/

was the main draw for the "disinherited."[74] The poor and insignificant could turn up to a Pentecostal church on a Sunday morning and be somebody because they could be used by God to bring a message to the congregation. The Charismatics were mainly middle class and already enjoyed a certain status in life. Merely exercising a gift was perhaps insufficient. The revival of the offices of prophet, and even apostle, was exciting to people of professional status.

A particular Classical Pentecostal twist has accentuated these key differences within the UK, though I have encountered what I am about to describe among Continental European Pentecostals too. Classical Pentecostals had some disagreements with the Apostolic Faith Church (AFC), or the "Apostolics" as they were known.[75] The AFC were a denomination within Classical Pentecostalism that were led by the notorious William Oliver Hutchinson who ended up believing that he was the "Manchild" of Revelation 12:13. The Apostolics also believed, like today's Apostolic Networks do, in the present day existence of apostles and prophets. Their denomination was led by the pronouncements of their prophets. The non-Apostolics, already beset with relentless bad press and opposition, were desperate to dissociate themselves from the Apostolics and so took up a stance on the gift of prophecy and the office of prophet that was as follows. Firstly, someone using the gift of prophecy may be termed a "prophet" in a relative sense, as Paul does in 1 Corinthians 14. However, a prophet in the fullest sense is an office-holder. Someone with the office of prophet may prophesy, but someone who prophesies is not necessarily a prophet or set to become one.[76] Secondly, neither prophets nor prophesiers are to give guidance. They may possibly predict (though this would be frowned upon) but they must never guide or lead. Acts 11:28; 13:1–3; and 21:10 are referenced in support. Gee was even more emphatic than Horton on this score: "It can be affirmed that there is not one single instance of the gift of prophecy being deliberately resorted to for guidance in the New Testament."[77] Thirdly, a sharp distinction was made between Old Testament prophets and New Testament prophets and prophesiers. The distinction is likened to priests:

---

74. Anderson, *Vision of the Disinherited*.

75. They are still in existence today, mainly in Wales, though the present-day denomination is rooted in a cessation from the extremists who followed Hutchinson.

76. So Gee, *Concerning Spiritual Gifts*, 58.

77. Ibid., 59.

in the Old Testament only a select few were priests; now, everyone is. On the basis of Peter's Day of Pentecost sermon, the same is said of prophets:[78]

> It is now the privilege of all believers to be personally led by the Spirit of God (Rom 8:14). It cannot be stated too emphatically that we need neither prophet nor priest to come between ourselves and the Lord in this present dispensation, and to submit for one moment to such a system is a definite step backwards into bondage.[79]

The net result of these stringencies was to effectively exclude the possibility of anyone today holding the office of prophet. If anyone did decide they are a prophet (and a further prohibition was placed on desiring to hold that office: we may eagerly desire to prophesy but not to be a prophet[80]), they would find that all they can legitimately do with it is prophesy in the same way as someone simply using the gift of prophecy. In other words, they may speak "edification, exhortation and comfort": three words (based on 1 Cor 14:3) that were held to be definitive and comprehensive.[81] Needless to say, Charismatics have showed none of these reservations and many ministries have thrived on being able to predict world events[82] and give very specific guidance.

Conclusion

Classical Pentecostalism, then, was birthed as the culmination of well over a hundred years of earnest longings for a more authentic Christian life: a life that was equipped to deal with the increasing moral pressures surrounding it, a faith that could articulate precisely the exact nature of its hope, ministry that could offer the tangible physical benefit of healing just like Jesus himself did, and worship that would be infused with restored New Testament gifts. It was an attempt at a reconstruction of Christianity in its original form. It was an end-time reply to an apostate world and to

---

78. All these points are elucidated at length by Horton, *Gifts of the Spirit*, 162–67.
79. Gee, *Concerning Spiritual Gifts*, 58.
80. Horton, *Gifts of the Spirit*, 162.
81. Ibid., 162, 164, 166.
82. For example, the Kansas City Prophet Paul Cain predicted that a revival would come to the UK in the Fall of 1990, and, more recently, a video in which Cindy Jacobs prophesied in a way suggestive of the devastating earthquake in the Phillipines: http://www.christianpost.com/news/prophecy-for-the-philippines-by-cindy-jacobs-video-goes-viral-animation-news-company-challenges-2009-predictions-108850/.

its formal religion. And its unsophisticated dogmas and straightforward expectations have written this vision onto the hearts of millions down to the present day.

Classical Pentecostalism and Charismatic faith are undoubtedly members of the same family. They are related but, in this family portrait, I want to bring out the unique qualities of the latter. To do this, I have not obliterated the face of Classical Pentecostalism but have here adjusted the light a little so that it falls more sharply and distinctly upon it. Now, as we come to look more closely upon the face of Charismatic Christianity we will see how different it is from its older cousin. It is more supple and quick to respond to new cultural phenomena. It is opportunist and often seems willing to make big compromises with historic Christian faith.

And it has behaved like this right from the start. We begin the story with its exploitation of the therapy culture of the sixties and seventies to create an entirely new expression of the Christian faith: the concept of Inner Healing.

2

Healing the Heart

THE INNER HEALING MOVEMENT

Inner Healing and the Origins the Charismatic Movement

In the 1960s, the Charismatic Renewal began contemporaneously with the Inner Healing Movement, and was part and parcel of it, but Inner Healing would go on to flourish best of all in the freedom afforded by the independent charismatic networks. Baptism in the Spirit had, by this point, become less than ever associated with any kind of sanctifying experience and was more or less synonymous with the experience of speaking in tongues for the first time, as exemplified by the rather matter-of-fact testimony of Charismatic Renewal's early leader, Dennis Bennett. So, something else was needed to fill the gap left by the evacuation of sanctification from the whole matrix of Pentecostal-Charismatic initiation. This came with the widespread circulation of Agnes Sanford's *The Healing Light*,[1] and other titles that soon followed. Sanford founded the Agnes Sanford School of Pastoral Care in 1958. John and Paula Sanford (disciples of, but not related to, Agnes Sanford) went on to found Elijah House Ministries in 1975. By 1977, Jimmy Carter's sister, Ruth Carter Stapleton (also influenced by Sanford), was making waves with an extensive speaking tour and her books *The Gift of Inner Healing* and *The Experience of Inner Healing*. Charismatic

---

1. Agnes Sanford, *Healing Light*. There is a book-length critique of Sanford's work: Gumprecht, *Abusing Memory: The Healing Theology of Agnes Sanford*.

expressions of Christianity went on to produce a succession of variations on this theme. In particular, the entrepreneurial 1980s saw the founding of Sozo Ministries, as well as the opening of Ellel Grange, the first of many centers for Ellel Ministries in the UK. Such ministries have continued to thrive, often in the face of much criticism, though they are rightly summarized as a "middle class phenomenon."[2] Most recently, alongside the psychoanalytic emphasis there has emerged more and more of a synthesis with cognitive-behavioral models. This begins to emerge in Theophostic Prayer Ministry and Bethel Sozo but comes to the fore most clearly in Freedom in Christ.

The Doctrine of Agnes Sanford

Influences

Alarmingly, Sanford is criticized for the same thing as the Word of Faith movement: the influence of New Thought philosophy, a mind-over-matter, transcendental philosophy originating in nineteenth century New England, alongside Christian Science, Unity, and other metaphysical cults. She is accused of ". . . almost single-handedly . . ." bringing "Jungian psychology and New Thought into the Christian church."[3] Sanford often acknowledged the profound influence of Dr. Emmet Fox and his *Sermon on the Mount*. Fox was reportedly a prominent figure within the Unity cult.[4] By the time she began her ministry, "New Thought assumptions permeated her books,"[5] a fact that she seemed not in the least ashamed of. She shared with these cults a basically pantheistic worldview: "He's in nature and He is nature."[6]

---

2. Velthuysen, "A Pastoral Theological Examination of Inner Healing," 2; See also Hunt, "Giving the Devil More Than His Due: Some Problems with Deliverance Ministry," in Osborn and Walker, *Harmful Religion*, 54–58

3. Gumprecht, *Abusing Memory*, 6.

4. Ibid.

5. Williams, *Spirit Cure*, 100.

6. Sanford *Healing Light*, 18; Sanford, *Healing Gifts of the Spirit*, 26–27; Sanford, *Sealed Orders*, 30. See discussion in Velthuysen, "Pastoral Theological Examination," 29–30.

The Use of Faith

Reading her book brings few surprises, perhaps because we have all grown so accustomed to hearing teaching that is similar. What does stand out is the way Sanford's work reflects the scientific worldview of the mid twentieth century, with which she tries to compete:

> The scientific attitude is the attitude of perfect meekness. . . . Through this meekness scientists have learned how to conform to the laws of nature, and by so doing have achieved great results. Through the same meekness those who seek God can produce results by learning to conform to His laws of faith and love.[7]

She recommends a four-part method: contact the power of God; turn it on; accept it by faith; finally, decide on some tangible thing to focus it on, some specific thing to ask God for. This she describes as a "prayer-project."[8] She refuses the fatalism of "Well, God's will be done,"[9] insisting that the instinctual desire in us is for life, to which the answer is to receive as much of God's life-giving Spirit as possible.[10] We must turn on "the light of God's creative energy."[11] Perhaps surprisingly, about half the book is about physical rather than emotional healing.

The Use of Visualization

A key aspect of Sanford's early teachings was the insistence on visualizing the healing. This she applied first to physical healing and then to other things such as being able to forgive someone by picturing them as a child of God and loved.[12] She set great store on the power of the mind to project love and wholeness, to the point where she believed that a new age was dawning that would eventually see an end to war because we have all learned the power of loving thoughts.[13] To one hospitalized G.I. she gave the following advice:

---

7. Sanford, *Healing Light*, 19.
8. Ibid., 21.
9. Ibid., 22.
10. Ibid.
11. Ibid., 28.
12. Ibid., passim.
13. Ibid., 60–62.

> . . . make a picture in your mind of the leg well. Shut your eyes and see it that way. See the bone all built in and the flesh strong and perfect around it. And play like you see a kind of light shining in it—a sort of a blue light, like one of these Neon signs, shining and burning and flowing all up and down the leg.[14]

Visualization soon caught on among practitioners of Inner Healing during the sixties and beyond, as evidenced by the following account of one such experience:

> I began to visualize myself as a boy of eight. I was startled to see . . . myself carrying a large bundle on my back, [which] apparently . . . symbolized my past needs and worries. "Now see if you can imagine Jesus appearing," she instructed. "Let him walk toward you." Much to my amazement, I—an ordained Reformed clergyman with a doctorate in psychology—found this happening to me. An image of Jesus moved slowly toward me out of that dark playground. He began to extend His hands toward me in a loving, accepting manner . . . I no longer was creating the scene. The figure of Christ reached over and lifted the bundle from my back. And he did so with such forcefulness that I literally sprang from the pew.[15]

Further Developments to the Present Day

The Healing of the Memories

The most controversial aspect of the Inner Healing Movement has been the doctrine of the "inner child" and the healing of the memories. Sanford came into contact with this teaching via her participation in the Camps Farthest Out gatherings of the 1960s. Francis McNutt made her see the importance of traumatic memories and the crucial process of letting these memories out of their repressed state. Sanford, in turn, propagated the idea via her *The Healing Gifts of the Spirit* of 1966. Here, she sells it by making it synonymous with the universally accepted Christian emphasis on the forgiveness of sins:

> The truth is that any wound to the soul so deep that it is not healed by our own self-searching and prayers is inevitably connected with a subconscious awareness of sin, either our own or our grievous

---

14. Ibid., 34.
15. Cited in Hunt and McMahon, *Seduction of Christianity*, 171–72.

reactions to the sins of others. The therapy that heals these wounds could be called the forgiveness of sins or it could be called the healing of memories.[16]

The healing of the memories would become associated especially with Ruth Carter Stapleton. However, this teaching ultimately derives from Hugh Misseldine's concept of the inner child,[17] which is a personification of a past hurt childhood. The pain could not be processed at the time because, as children, we lack the emotional and rational skills that an adult has. The pain then gets parked somewhere within our unconscious mind, and consequently proves difficult to access as an adult, even though it may be showing itself in all manner of neurotic behavior. Talk therapy is the commonest way of accessing it, hence there is an issue with the power of suggestion. There is a tendency in patients undergoing guided talk therapy towards "retrospective falsification and fabrication."[18] The therapist can cause the client to supposedly remember incidents that he or she thinks the counselor is looking for.[19] Writing as the movement matured, Seamands offered clear cautions that the healing of the memories approach was not for everyone but specifically for those that have repressed painful memories. These memories are so repressed that, without therapy, the patient is strongly unwilling, and effectively unable, to remember them without help.[20] Either way, the goal of the healing process is that, in time, the painful events from the past could be routinely recalled by the patient, but without feeling any pain.[21]

Beyond the doctrine of the inner child there is, both in Sanford and most other practitioners, a general acceptance of the insights of psychoanalysis, especially of the Jungian variety. This use of selected insights from psychology, coupled with a simplistic use of Scripture in support, is often criticized, and sometimes with good reason, as naively applied.[22]

16. Sanford, *Healing Gifts of the Spirit*, 110.

17. Missildine, *Your Inner Child of the Past*.

18. Jackson, "Stapleton," 195. Like Gumprecht's critique of Sanford, Jackson felt that Stapleton was influenced by "cultic theologies" and even Buddhism: 195.

19. Jackson, "Stapleton," 195. See also, Yapko, *Suggestions of Abuse*, and Dineen, *Manufacturing Victims*.

20. Seamands, *Healing of Memories*, 188.

21. E.g., Sanford, *Sealed Orders*, 196.

22. Velthuysen, "Pastoral Theological Examination," 10. As with any new combinations of things, the results of the synthesis are sometimes quite striking. Sanford, for instance, articulates a fascinating understanding of the atonement using the language

This basically psychoanalytical approach has persisted down to the present day and is an important component in Bethel Sozo Prayer Ministry, which was founded in 1998 by Dawna DaSilva and Teresa Liebscher of Bethel Church, and Theophostic Prayer Ministry, also started in 1998, by Ed Smith,[23] though in both cases the psychoanalytic approach is not the only approach used. Let us take a quick sample of the techniques employed.

Bethel Sozo

A Sozo session lasts for between an hour and a half and three hours and involves a team of two counselors plus the "Sozee," the client of the ministry. It is always two women for one female sozee or two men for one male sozee. There are currently no academic critiques of Bethel Sozo, though there are plenty of conservative cult-watching critics of the usual kind. Most of the information I have is through contact with participants and via the resources made publically available by Bethel Sozo, which are scattered here and there.

When a sozee goes to be "Sozo'd," the main tool that they will encounter is the "four doors" approach borrowed from a technique pioneered in Argentina in the early nineties. The participant is asked to picture four doors: the sexual sin door, the occult door, the hatred and bitterness door, and the fear and unmet needs door. They are asked: "which one is open?" or "which one is open the widest?" It is the belief that all of the troubles we battle with are because of the entrance of sin via one of these open doors.

Other tools that are usually included in a session are:

1. The Father Ladder: A Trinitarian meditation in which faulty perceptions either of the Father (because of earthly fathers), the Son (because of siblings or friends), or the Holy Spirit (because of earthly mothers) are corrected. Sozees are asked to describe, "How do you see or sense Father God. Holy Spirit . . . Jesus?"[24]

---

and concepts of Carl Jung: "[Jesus] entered into the collective unconscious of the human race, into the mind of every person." Sanford, *Healing Gifts of the Spirit*, 101.

23. Smith, "History of TPM." A detailed evaluation of TPM is here: Miller, "An Evaluation of Theophostic Prayer Ministry." http://theophostic.com/resources/1/pdf/PST001.pdf.

24. Reese, "Basic Sozo Training Version 2.0."

2. The Wall: The sozee is asked to visualize the barriers and hindrances that separate them from God.
3. Presenting Jesus. The Truth is a person: Jesus, and in the prayer ministry session, Jesus is invited to speak his truth into areas where lies have been believed. The Sozee asks: "Jesus, help me to perceive your presence," or "Jesus, what do you want me to know?"[25]

Theophostic / Transformation Prayer Ministry

Recently, the name of this ministry has changed to Transformation Prayer Ministry, though the principles appear similar to the original Theophostic Prayer Ministry. Founder Ed Smith explained Theophostic Prayer Ministry as follows:

> Theo (God) Phostic (light) is a ministry of prayer that is Christ centered and God reliant for its direction and outcome. Simply stated, it is encouraging a person to discover and expose what he believes that is a falsehood; and then encouraging him to have an encounter with Jesus Christ through the Holy Spirit in prayer, thus allowing the Lord to reveal His truth to the wounded person's heart and mind.

He is very clear that, "The process is God directed. Anytime the counselor seeks to direct or guide what is happening in the mind of the person, what they do ceases to be *TheoPhostic* counseling."[26] There is no technique except that, despite the claim to not be offering guidance, the counselor does provide a series of cues while the client is in a state of prayerful waiting on God: "I asked her to imagine herself . . . I led him to locate . . . I asked him to drift back . . . I asked her to close her eyes and focus. . . . Focus on that scared feeling . . . Focus on that thought. . . . Focus on this hurt. . . . Let Him place His hand on your chest . . . I asked them to sense the presence of Jesus and listen. . . . I encouraged them to speak whatever they hear . . ."[27]

---

25. Reese, "Basic Sozo Training," 9.

26. Smith, *Beyond Tolerable Recovery*, 112. There have been numerous updates since the 1996 edition, in which the word "ministry" replaces the word "counselling," in order to emphasize the non-directive nature of this method. See also his book: *Healing Life's Hurts*.

27. Smith, *Beyond Tolerable Recovery*, 43–45, 52, 58, 73, 77, critiqued in Bobgan and Bobgan, *TheoPhostic Counseling*, 69–72.

The purpose of these cues is to invite the client to feel again the pain of their hurt, but then, in the midst of the full awfulness of the pain, to feel the presence of Jesus intruding upon it.

Theophostic / Transformation Prayer Ministry draws from cognitive-behavioral therapy, there being an emphasis on the power of believing lies. Smith confidently asserts: "It is possible to believe and receive God's forgiveness, reconciliation, and eternal life and yet live one's life totally in bondage to the lies of one's childhood."[28]

This approach is ultimately indebted to Albert Ellis, the father of cognitive-behavioral approaches. Almost all of Ellis's ideas in turn are an outworking of a single aphorism that he discovered in the writings of the Greek Stoic philosopher Epictetus: "It is not events that disturb people, it is their judgments concerning them."[29] It was not the events of our past that automatically led to trauma and disturbance, it was the lie that we believed about ourselves at that point which did all the damage: "Cognitive therapies maintain that behavior and emotions result largely from one's appraisal of the situation, and that, because appraisal is influenced by beliefs, assumptions, images, and self-talk, these cognitions become targets of therapy."[30]

Bethel Sozo, Transformation Prayer Ministry, and Freedom in Christ (to come) all agree with this fundamental post-psychoanalytical insight.

So, to sum up the Theophostic approach:

1. Feel the pain
2. Relive the memory
3. Expose the lie that was believed[31]

---

28. Smith, *Beyond Tolerable Recovery*, 185.

29. Epictetus, *Enchiridion*, 5. See Ellis and MacLaren, *Rational Emotive Behavior Therapy*, 32–33.

30. Corsini and Auerbach, *Concise Encyclopedia of Psychology*, 133. Similarly, in Theophostic Prayer Ministry, Smith insists that, though it is historic experiences that are behind ongoing difficulties in the lives of Christians, it is not the experience itself but the interpretation that was placed upon it—which usually takes the form of a lie—that creates all the problems: Maier and Monroe, "Theological Analysis," 177. This tendency to misinterpret life is, according to Smith, a product of the way we as children tended to misinterpret things but also a product of our infantile gullibility to the interpretations of adults and of Satan himself that were suggested to us: Maier and Monroe, "A Theological Analysis," 177.

31. "We understand Smith to mean that when a person experiences the utter darkness of the lie, they will be in such a place as to be able to hear the contrasting light of God's truth." Maier and Monroe, "Theological Analysis," 174n28.

4. Receive God's truth or light that deals with the lie and heals the pain.[32]

Ingeniously, any criticism of Smith's ministry is itself put down to the childhood hurts of the critic,[33] though he has recently been very cooperative with a lengthy investigation by the Christian Research Institute.[34] Possibly the main complaint has been the exaggerated claims made by Smith about his technique's efficacy.[35] Smith also makes exaggerated claims about the prevalence of the need for therapy, estimating unusually high rates of people in churches that have been abused in some way or other as children.[36]

Theophostic Prayer Ministry, in common with Bethel Sozo, uses the term "prayer ministry" in order to avoid the legal minefield that would result from claiming clinical competence as a therapy. Research on the efficacy of these non-professional alternatives is still in its infancy though early indications seem to suggest that these are no less effective than the professional services of qualified therapists.[37]

Freedom in Christ

Neil Anderson has written numerous books about finding spiritual freedom. Perhaps the most notable is his, *The Bondage Breaker*.[38] This book alone has attracted a very lengthy critique from Christian Discernment Ministries. The dominant metaphors in his writings are those of bondage-breaking and stronghold-busting rather than healing. He desires that the truth would set people free of compulsive, self-destructive behaviors. He tends not to tackle substance and alcohol addiction but focuses more on sexual and emotional problems, seeing the answer to almost everything as being to simply believe the truth about yourself rather than believing

---

32. "Once you 'know the truth,' you cannot go back into the lie." The healing is "maintenance free." From a cassette recording of Smith referenced in Maier and Monroe, "Theological Analysis," 174.

33. Christian Discernment, "Theophostic Theology," 3.

34. The full report of 2005 is here: http://theophostic.com/resources/1/pdf/PST001.pdf.

35. E.g., Entwistle, "Shedding Light on Theophostic Ministry 2," 35–42.

36. Critiqued in Entwistle, "Shedding Light on Theophostic Ministry 1," 26–34.

37. E.g., Garzon et al., who emphasize the very provisional nature of their findings: "Freedom in Christ," 41–51.

38. Anderson, *Bondage Breaker*.

what either people or the devil have told you. From the very beginning of the course, participants are avidly encouraged to describe themselves as saints rather than sinners. This sets the tone for the whole approach, which is that we behave in accordance with what we believe to be the truth about ourselves. Behavior follows belief, rather than the other way round. Participants are asked to speak the truth *until* they believe it. Yet, throughout the course and despite the rigors of stronghold-busting affirmations that must be repeated every day for several weeks, the approach is likened to simply switching on the light rather than trying to fight the darkness. Freedom is sold as something effortless but taught as though achieved only with considerable effort.

All turns upon the achievement of a kind of New Testament version of healthy self-esteem and concepts related to that. Echoing Maslow's hierarchy of needs, a lot hangs upon how well we have understood that we are significant, secure and accepted.[39] The main means of moving into these liberating truths is, as mentioned above, to speak out positive affirmations. In the case of stronghold busting, it is recommended that the daily repetition of affirmations should go on for up to six weeks.[40] A typical affirmation will involve two elements: renouncing and announcing: "I renounce the lie that . . .," and "I announce the truth that . . ."

Anderson's methodology for *Freedom in Christ* has attracted some criticism, largely owing to the fact that, while the underlying theology aims to base itself on the New Testament letters, the methodology appears to be a hybrid between Charismatic teachings about self-deliverance and the techniques of cognitive-behavioral psychology.[41] It is not unique in this, organizations such as Ellel Ministries having taken a similar approach in respect to demonology. The combination of the demonological and psychological in *Freedom in Christ* leads to an inconsistency in the material. The main *Freedom in Christ* booklet that participants work through in conjunction with a DVD, makes it clear that the enemies to our freedom in Christ are "the world, the flesh and the devil."[42] Behavioral psychology dominates this part. Then, after week nine, participants are introduced to another booklet called, *The Steps to Freedom in Christ*. In this booklet the

---

39. Anderson and Goss, *Freedom in Christ*, 14.

40. Ibid., 81.

41. The most comprehensive critiques have been online articles from Elliot Miller, e.g., "Bondage Maker: Examining the Message and Method of Neil T. Anderson."

42. Anderson and Goss, *Freedom in Christ*, 35–62.

emphasis shifts to the devil, with many of the renunciations being about, or even directed at, the devil and demons. This is due to Anderson's view of how a sin-confess-cycle is broken. It is simply this: "Submit to God, resist the devil and he will flee from you" (James 4:7). The seven *Steps to Freedom* are designed to be the point at which that is actually happening in the life of every participant.[43]

> No matter how difficult your life might be, there is great news for you. You are not a helpless victim caught between two nearly equal but opposite heavenly super-powers. Satan is a liar and a deceiver, and the only way he can have power over you is if you believe his lies.[44]

Serious research into the long term efficacy of Freedom in Christ is lacking but an initial probe, published in 2001, revealed positive indicators, especially in terms of reduced anxiety and raised self-esteem. However, the paper does not deal with a claim that recurs in the popular blog appraisals of FIC, namely that the effects are temporary.[45]

Conclusion

Inner Healing methodologies, like some of the other Charismatic distinctives we will be looking at, are syncretistic. I will be more critical of some of these syncretisms than others but these syncretisms, in my view, are not to be written off simply because they are a mixture of things from a variety of sources. They have not led us, as Hunt and McMahon[46] feared, into the New Age movement, nor as John MacArthur Jr. claimed and still claims into "chaos."[47] Neither is it adequate to assess the merits of a given practice solely on the grounds of the notoriously loaded question: "Is this biblical?" A better question perhaps might be framed by the discipline of biblical theology. That discipline might ask, "Is this in line with a biblical worldview?" We would immediately note such things as the individualism and self-absorption that might seem to be encouraged, and that these methods do not obviously allow the participant to claim responsibility for

43. Anderson, *Steps to Freedom in Christ*.
44. Ibid., 9.
45. Garzon et al., "Freedom in Christ," 41–51.
46. Hunt and McMahon, *Seduction of Christianity*.
47. MacArthur, *Charismatic Chaos*. MacArthur, *Strange Fire*.

their behavior.[48] More positively, it could be said that salvation history in the biblical narrative has as its goal the healing of humanity and the image of God restored there, but I am boring myself already.

Far more interesting is to better define what is actually going on here. For one thing, as has often enough been pointed out, engagement with elements within Western culture (such as psychotherapy) can often mean engagement with elements that already possess "an unstated or understated Judaeo-Christian value scheme."[49] John Milbank is against "correlationist" theologies which capitulate to secular modernity. Our ways of interacting with the world must be, as James K. A. Smith puts it, ". . . distinctively Christian at their foundation,"[50] but Milbank is equally clear that secular culture, despite its pretentions to religious neutrality, is deeply indebted to historic Christianity and sees itself as Christianity's eschatological destination.[51] Hence, Radical Orthodoxy, "attempts to reclaim the world by situating its concerns and activities within a theological framework."[52] It weaves back into Christianity elements from secular culture that are understood to truly belong to the faith.[53] Is there any harm then in retrieving and reclaiming secular bits and pieces and rehydrating them for Christian use, situating them within a theological framework? It all depends, of course, on how well this is done. It depends whether it is done in a way that "liquidates"[54] Christian religion and reduces it to the criteria of the secular system it has aligned itself with, or whether it truly entails "a thinking out of the resources of revelation alone."[55]

The practitioners we first looked at took the insights of Freud and Jung and noted their emphasis upon a person's past as key to their healing. From their biblical worldview, these practitioners noticed that when the Bible addresses the past therapeutically it places forgiveness at the center. So this was what they did: Sanford, Carter Stapleton, and Seamands took

---

48. Bulle, *God Wants You Rich*, 176–82.
49. Maroney, *Religious Syncretism*, 165.
50. Smith, *Introducing Radical Orthodoxy*, 42.
51. E.g., Milbank, *Theology and Social Theory*, 9–10. Secular sociology ". . . fulfils the destiny of Christianity . . ."
52. Milbank, Pickstock, and Ward, *Radical Orthodoxy*, 1.
53. Smith, "What Hath Cambridge."
54. Ward, *True Religion*, 36.
55. Milbank, *Word Made Strange*, 36.

psychoanalysis and Christianized it by putting forgiveness at the center, and even invented a brand new technical term to describe the thing they were seeking to address: "unforgiveness." Then, as the fashion in therapy moved away from psychoanalytical ideas, a new generation of practitioners such as Dawna DaSilva and Teresa Liebscher, Ed Smith and Neil Anderson simply added into the existing mix the new cognitive-behavioral insights. This was extremely easy as Epictetus and Ellis could simply be replaced by Christ in John 8:32 saying, "You shall know the truth and the truth shall make you free." Simplistic though this is, is any of this really "Psychotheological Naiveté"?[56]

The only point at which syncretism becomes a danger is when, in the service of amalgamating aspects of two different traditions the Christian element "loses basic structure and identity."[57] Inner Healing ideas can do violence to Reformed Christian soteriology. Inner Healing tends to require of that tradition a complete rethink of its doctrine of sin and seems to replace sanctification with something unrecognizably different. From an Eastern Orthodox viewpoint, however, there are fewer difficulties. Indeed Derek Flood has recently written very ably a view of the Christian gospel message that redefines it, in the light of Irenaeus, Athanasius, and other Eastern fathers, as healing.[58]

Another thing to point out is that all religion is syncretistic. This is partly down to what Newbigin recognized,[59] which is that the gospel always expresses itself through a particular culture. A culturally neutral version of the faith has never existed. But also, research in the history of religions seems to demonstrate that the aspiration to doctrinal purity in any religion is, to a great extent, misguided.[60] Rather it is the very tendency to change and adapt in an eclectic or even chaotic way that has been the very key

---

56. Jackson, "Stapleton," 195–97.

57. Schrieter, *Constructing Local Theologies*, 144. As far as Schreiter is concerned, this is what a syncretism essentially is. "Syncretism . . . has to do with the mixing of elements of two religious systems to the point where at least one, if not both, of the systems loses basic structure and identity."

58. Flood, *Healing the Gospel*. Many of the contributors to *Stricken by God?* also draw from this rich Eastern tradition of theosis: Jersak and Hardin, *Stricken by God? Nonviolent Identification and the Victory of Christ*.

59. Michael Goheen has supplied a remarkably succinct and compelling account of Newbigin's thought here: http://qideas.org/articles/the-lasting-legacy-of-lesslie-newbigin/.

60. So Maroney, *Religious Syncretism*, 167–75.

to survival for the most successful world religions, especially Christianity. Syncretism is a healthy and normal, if faltering and fallible, response to seasons of rapid cultural change. Inner Healing has been exactly that, and hopefully, a few people have been healed along the way.

Excursus

The Shop Window
The Rise of Charismatic Worship

A Brief History

Charismatic worship has become the default setting in the majority of evangelical churches, especially in Britain,[1] and this regardless of whether the church in question is a Charismatic evangelical church or not. By anyone's reckoning, such near ubiquity in the space of five decades, is a remarkable achievement: a phenomenal ruse of a religious subculture. Briefly, here is the story of how this came to be so.

The angle here is somewhat UK-centric. This is because much of the material began life as lectures in a UK context, but hopefully I have painted a picture which is of broad appeal and usefulness.

The Advent of the Chorus

In the latter half of the nineteenth century, at the height of the all-time peak in the production of evangelical hymns, a slightly new phase in the history of sung worship began. It started with the despised and deeply eccentric Salvation Army. They pioneered the idea of the chorus of a hymn being sung out on the streets without the verses. This added a note of immediacy.

---

1. Ward, *Selling Worship*, 1.

The choruses were catchy and easily remembered. The Army went on to write a number of choruses that would never have any verses and thus were no longer hymns in the truest sense, they were choruses. Coupled with this was the popularization of the Negro spiritual, a similarly immediate, memorable style of worship, to which the roots of black gospel music (and hence, pop music itself) can be traced.

The Coffee Bar Outreaches

However, as recently as the 1950s, neither the chorus nor the Negro spiritual was by any means ubiquitous in the churches and it was only the emergence of youth culture during the late fifties and sixties that forced the issue. New kinds of song, written and performed by Christian beat groups, needed to come forth if a new generation was to be reached with the gospel in a relevant way. Evangelicals were quick to make use of the new coffee bar culture of the youth. In Britain these became the main venue for music-based outreach, which, by December 1964, had organized itself into the organization Musical Gospel Outreach,[2] under the auspices of Pete Meadows and others, and later bolstered by the celebrity status of Cliff Richard at events it hosted such as Spree 1973. The songs commonly in use were compiled into a song book: the Anglican *Youth Praise Book One* in 1966. Despite the title, most of the songs were not worship songs but were songs designed for evangelistic performance.

The Jesus Movement

The Jesus Movement consisted of disenchanted hippies who, towards the end of the sixties and into the early seventies, had withdrawn from the free love of flower power to embrace an evangelical and charismatic brand of Christianity. But they continued to seek to express themselves using the norms of their subculture, including rock music. Larry Norman was the leading example of this. The music coming out of this movement was still not as yet worship-orientated. Instead, these were typically protest songs written from a faith perspective. The Jesus People were inimical to

---

2. This eventually became Kingsway Music.

all institutions, including the church, so tended to pioneer their brand of spirituality and music in a way distinct from the mainstream.[3]

The Charismatic Renewal

At the same time, since 1960 in the USA, and since 1965 in the UK, a movement had been gathering pace within the older denominations that was seeing thousands of people enter into experiences normally associated with the Pentecostals, namely, the Baptism in the Holy Spirit and the manifestation of the Gifts of the Spirit. With most of the Jesus People also experiencing these same phenomena, it was almost inevitable[4] that there would be a coming together of the two streams of evangelical-charismatic youth subculture and the wider all-age Charismatic Renewal which was seeking freer means of expressing worship. From around 1970 onwards, it was clear, too, that not all of these new Charismatics had stayed within their denominations but, like the Jesus People in the USA, thousands had left their denominations and gathered in independent house groups. In the early seventies, these soon gathered themselves around key apostolic figures such as the Fort Lauderdale Five in America or Wally North, Bryn and Keri Jones, and Gerald Coates in the UK.

In America, Jimmy and Carol Owens had begun to develop a resource appropriate to the needs of all Charismatics.[5] Their *Come Together* musical came to Britain under the auspices of Jean Darnell (a Renewalist) and Gerald Coates (a Restorationist) in 1973. The record achieved sales of 57,869 in Britain alone within three years, making it, at that time, the bestselling Christian record of all time in the UK.[6]

With *Come Together* we start to see the introduction of some of the classic physical actions for which Charismatic Worship would become so well known: "If you can't quite accept the freedom to lift your hands high

---

3. Williams, "Charismatic Worship," in Engle and Basden, *Exploring the Worship Spectrum*, 141.

4. Despite Ward's claim that this development was "neither obvious nor natural," *Selling Worship*, 1.

5. Writing from a US perspective, Williams dates the appearance of folk music styles and the resulting "more sustained periods of free worship" in the Charismatic Renewal to the mid-1960s, linking this development to the genre created by the anti-Vietnam and civil rights protest songs. Williams, "Charismatic Worship," in Engle and Basden, *Exploring the Worship Spectrum*, 141.

6. Ward, *Selling Worship*, 53.

in praise and blessing to the Lord," suggest Jimmy and Carol Owens, "try cupping them in front of you like a vessel ready to receive an outpouring of living water from the Lord."[7] Bebbington records his observations of his home church in Nottingham: Queensbury Street Baptist Church. This church became part of the Renewal in the seventies. In successive return visits to the church, he notes numbers of people raising their hands during worship: "2 in 1978, 8 in 1988, 20 at the start of 1989 and 30 at the end of the year."[8] All of this was in the context of a culture that was becoming more and more preoccupied with "the use of the body."[9]

Following hot on the heels of *Come Together* was the songbook *Sound of Living Waters* in 1974,[10] followed by *Fresh Sounds* in 1976.[11] Very popular at the time, and dominating the songs in both collections were Houston based Christian folk band the Fisherfolk. Betty Pulkingham, one of the compilers of the collection, was married to Graham Pulkingham who had experienced the baptism in the Spirit via David Wilkerson in 1966. Together they led the hugely successful Church of the Redeemer, as well as a commune called Community of Celebration. The Fisherfolk were born out of the worship of the Church of the Redeemer in Houston.

Undoubtedly, it was the rapid spread of this worship music that helped the Charismatic Renewal to take hold.[12] The incorporation of musical styles that were in tune with the ballads and folk revival songs of the early seventies created "a religion for ex-hippies who now had children and straight jobs."[13]

Restoration

Restoration is the term used to describe the "come outers": those Charismatics (in the UK at least) who left their denominations to form independent

---

7. From the *Come Together* booklet of 1972, cited in Ward, *Selling Worship*, 52.

8. Bebbington, "Evangelicals and Public Worship," 16. The thought of him sitting at the back, hunched over his notebook, while he frantically counts hands each time *Shine, Jesus, Shine!* gets to the chorus is a bit sad, though I must confess to having done not dissimilar research myself.

9. Bebbington, "Evangelicals and Public Worship," 17.

10. Pulkingham and Harper, *Sound of Living Waters*.

11. Pulkingham and Harper, *Fresh Sounds*.

12. So Ward, *Selling Worship*, 59, citing the Anglican report by the General Synod: *The Charismatic Movement in the Church of England*, 10.

13. Ward, *Growing Up Evangelical*, 126.

house churches. These house churches in turn organized themselves into informal networks with a distinctive ecclesiology. Many of these, such as New Frontiers are still thriving and growing and are now mostly referred to as Apostolic Networks, a term derived from the strong attachment within these groups to the five Eph 4:11 ministries, especially apostles and prophets.

Pete Ward somewhat downplays the contribution of British Restorationism to Charismatic worship and seems write with relish about its eventual outflanking by Vineyard[14] and Spring Harvest.[15] Yet its contribution is not to be underestimated. The landmark songbook of 1981, *Songs of Fellowship Volume 1*, which was dominated by songs emerging from the Restoration networks, set the tone of worship for the rest of the decade, contributing some of the most enduring and influential songs of the whole movement.[16] The output from Restoration tended to come from various, speaker-singer partnerships: Dave Fellingham (with Terry Virgo/New Frontiers), Noel Richards—plus Dave Bilbrough—(with Gerald Coates/ Pioneer), Graham Kendrick (with Roger Forster/Ichthus), Chris Bowater (with Stuart Bell/Ground Level), and Dave Haddon (Bryn Jones/Harvestime). Also emerging from New Frontiers in future years would be Paul Oakley, Stuart Townend, and Lou Fellingham, and from Pioneer, Martin Smith of Cutting Edge, and Delirious? fame.[17]

Restoration seems to have pioneered the beginnings of a theology of Charismatic Worship, based mainly on the quotation in Acts 15:16–17 of Amos 9:11–12. This speaks of the rebuilding of the tabernacle of David. Writing in 1980, Ron Trudinger of Salt and Light explained:

> In striking contrast to the tent in the wilderness, Mount Zion was characterized by continual free celebration and worship, often noisy, around the ark. Similarly, in striking contrast to most traditional settings, a Spirit led congregation today engages in open praise and worship.[18]

14. Ward, *Selling Worship*, 100.

15. Ibid., 71.

16. Described by Scotland as "contrastingly raucous in tone" compared to *Come Together*, *Sound of Living Water* and *Fresh Sounds*: Scotland, *Charismatics and the Next Millennium*, 56.

17. The story of the origins and rise to success of Cutting Edge and Delirious? is told in Ward, *Selling Worship*, 114.

18. Trudinger, *Master Plan*, 36. This was brought to my attention by Nigel Scotland *Charismatics and the Next Millennium*, 55–56 who describes this theology as having

The Shop Window

Vineyard and the Renewal of the Renewal

It is difficult to exaggerate the significance of the visit of John Wimber to two Anglican churches in 1981. Due to a friendship with David Watson of St Michael le Belfrey in York, Wimber secured invitations to Holy Trinity Brompton from Sandy Millar and to St Andrews Chorleywood by Bishop David Pytches.[19] Everyone knew of his emphasis on signs and wonders but his style of worship made easily as much of an impact. Congregations found themselves caught up in a seamless succession of very simple yet touching and intimate songs that were all addressed *to* Jesus rather than being *about* him. This new style transformed the face of Charismatic worship, dramatically reducing the declarative and triumphalist emphasis and introducing a tone of "subliminal eroticism." The songs of the Vineyard were all written in the style of a romantic ballad, and made free use of the idioms commonly used to describe the love between a man and a woman in love songs. Not surprisingly, these were a good deal mellower than the triumphalist anthems of Restoration, reflecting very much the laid back ministry style of Wimber himself.

The impact upon these two churches was so great that a number of significant new ministries were birthed that have gone from strength to strength. St Andrews Chorleywood produced New Wine. In turn, the need to provide a dedicated youth arm to New Wine brought forth Soul Survivor and the Survivor Church in Watford. Out of the Soul Survivor events, the ministry of Matt Redman, who had been the teenage worship leader at Chorleywood, became prominent, taking on international dimensions in the 1990s. Meanwhile, Nicky Gumbel of Holy Trinity Brompton developed the Alpha course, his calling having come to a large extant as a result of receiving ministry from Wimber. More recently, Tim Hughes's worship ministry there has achieved international acclaim.

Wimber himself said this about worship:

> We are headed towards one goal: intimacy with God. I define intimacy as belonging to or revealing one's deepest nature to another (in this case God), and it is marked by close association, presence and contact.[20]

"much to commend it."

19. His impact on Terry Virgo and New Frontiers was also significant: Price, "Wonder of Wimber," 7.

20. Wimber, "Worship: Intimacy with God," 5.

Spring Harvest and the Mainstreaming of Charismatic Worship

Spring Harvest resulted from the teaming up of British Youth for Christ and *Buzz Magazine* to produce the first Spring Harvest event in Prestatyn, Wales, in 1979, attracting 3,000 people. In future years attendance would grow to 80,000 (1990) and be divided into more than one event. Graham Kendrick was the main worship leader at the early events and was able to use it as a platform for promoting his first and subsequent albums devoted entirely to worship music.[21] Despite this, Ward[22] agrees with Walker[23] that Spring Harvest was probably the biggest reason for the gradual sidelining of the contribution of Restoration networks. People could, after all, enjoy the same energy and excitement in Spring Harvest worship without having to go to a Restorationist Bible Week or church and be subjected to its exclusivist and authoritarian tendencies. In fact, you didn't even need to be a Charismatic to enjoy Spring Harvest.

Soul Survivor, Hillsong, Hillsong United, Chris Tomlin, Jesus Culture

The story of the last three decades has been one of progressively more performance-orientated expressions of Charismatic Worship. In fact, the songs now in circulation combined with the mega-church and big event cultures that form their natural habitat, can scarcely any longer be described as "Charismatic" in any biblical sense. Hillsong seems to be the high water mark of this tendency. It is a movement that is well rehearsed at replicating its brand across the world, and its worship product is slickly packaged and exported, though this is not to cast doubts on the sincerity of its content.

There is an interesting trend once again towards appealing to youth, just as there was at the very start. In fact, at present the Charismatic Worship music scene is dominated by songs coming out of youth ministries, specifically: Soul Survivor, Hillsong United, Chris Tomlin, and Jesus Culture. Any glance at the number of hits that some Hillsong United clips have acquired on YouTube is an indicator of the considerable success this genre

---

21. Ward, *Selling Worship*, 71.
22. Ibid., 72.
23. Walker, *Restoring the Kingdom*, 309.

continues to enjoy. Chris Tomlin's album sales continue to hold their own against non-Christian competitors on the Bilboard 200.[24]

Evaluations

Obscelesence

One of the most common criticisms of Charismatic worship songs, though this is not necessarily a weakness, is that they are here today, gone tomorrow. The sheer transitoriness and disposability of Christian worship songs today is unprecedented, with only a tiny minority showing any evidence of standing the test of time. For the most part, a song has currency within a church culture for perhaps no more than a year, after which it starts to sound tired. Chris Bowater of Ground Level would explain this transience as being part and parcel of the prophetic qualities of Charismatic worship: "My writing was birthed in a prophetic environment. . . . Kingdom and Restoration theology produces a prophetic edge,"[25] though he also laments the fact that the initial prophetic imperative to produce songs that were the "word of the Lord" for a particular time or season of church life, quickly degenerated into a rat race to produce the next album.[26] The commercial reasons for a song's rapid obscelesence, then, seem to have largely taken over from the prophetic reasons.

Narcissism

Matt Redman could be one of Charismatic Worship's most outspoken critics from within, and is clear about the dangers of pride: "One trend in worship which increasingly worries me," says Redman, "is the whole performance thing. . . . Praise is a contradiction of pride. Pride says, 'Look at me,' but praise longs for people to see Jesus."[27] He, along with Mike Pilavachi, was

---

24. His 2013 album *Burning Lights* reached the No. 1 spot: http://www.billboard.com/biz/articles/news/1490583/chris-tomlin-scores-first-no-1-album-on-billboard-200-chart.

25. Email from Chris Bowater to Anne Dyer dated 4/13/2005, reported in Dyer, "Some Theological Trends," 38.

26. Bowater, *A Believer's Guide to Worship*, 61, cited in Dyer, "Some Theological Trends," 39.

27. Redman, *Unquenchable Worshipper*, 66.

at the heart of "ban the band"[28] experiments at Survivor Church that have been replicated elsewhere. A tendency is for the worshippers to act as consumers placing the band under ever increasing pressure to perform, to produce the ultimate worship experience. The band can then find themselves responding to this demand by the use of "hype," defined by Scotland as "to stir up or artificially contrive to raise the intensity level of worship or prayer," including raising the volume, the use of repetition and encouraging clapping and foot stomping.[29] The result is that everyone goes home feeling drained. This situation can spiral until it is time to ban the band and have a season of spontaneous free contributions from the congregation.

Eroticism

Eroticism in Christian worship is nothing new. Ever since Bernard of Clairvaux wrote his sermons on the Song of Songs, the Bride and Bridegroom metaphor has been resorted to repeatedly. Female mystics such as Catherine of Siena and Julian of Norwich reveled in this style of spirituality. Martin Luther,[30] Count Zinzendorf,[31] and the Moravians[32] continued in the Bridal mysticism tradition as well as exploring other ways of expressing their deep-seated love for Jesus. The Moravians in particular caused much offence with the publication of their first English language hymnal of 1749, which contained some overt eroticism.[33] Though reigned in later on, many of the eighteenth and early nineteenth century hymn writers have been noted for similar erotic content, a precedent that seems to have been set by Isaac Watts' use, again, of the Song of Songs.[34]

Martyn Percy's study of the worship he witnessed at Toronto Airport Vineyard Church in the mid-1990s takes criticism of this type of content to an entirely new level.[35] While most commentators on Charismatic Worship

---

28. Ward, *Selling Worship*, 172. Also Jarrod Cooper's emphasis on going back to basics: Cooper, *Glory in the Church*, 15, cited in Dyer, "Theological Trends," 45.

29. Scotland, *Charismatics and the Next Millennium*, 61.

30. In his *Freedom of the Christian Man*, discussed in Westerholm, *Perspectives Old and New on Paul*, 31.

31. E.g., *Nine Public Lectures on Important Subjects in Religion*, 24–33.

32. Stead and Stead, *The Exotic Plant*, 325.

33. Ibid., 266.

34. De Jong, "'I Want to be Like Jesus,'" 465–66.

35. Percy, "Sweet Rapture," 71–106.

are empathetic to some degree, Percy is openly hostile and relentless. He defines the whole Charismatic movement as centered on an ideology of "sublimated eroticism."[36] He claims that this fundamental shared belief system is expressed in songs "packed with images and analogies of intimacy, immediacy, power and eroticism," and that this is what actually causes the various physical manifestations that were particularly in evidence at Toronto Airport Vineyard at that time.[37] He makes comparisons with ancient Greek Dionysian worship with its use of rhythm leading to ecstasy.[38] He describes Charismatic worship of the Vineyard variety as "mood-enhancing" and almost "smoochy."[39] He notes, as I will shortly, that "the cross of Christ is almost absent."[40] The ideology of the worship is, according to Percy, summed up in the word "You" addressed directly to God, and the use of the word "Lord." Together these titles focus the worshippers on the love and power of God respectively.[41] He notes, with some degree of cynicism, the appeal of this brand of worship to women, specifically middle-aged married women: the same social group that are the target of articles in women's magazines about how to inject some romance back into their love lives.[42] When the content of the songs is combined with observations about the women's quasi-orgasmic behavior, it is easy for him to agree with a casual observation made by a visitor to Holy Trinity Brompton at the height of the Toronto Blessing: "it looked to me like a lot of women having orgasms, led by a man at the front."[43] He concludes that Charismatic Worship, of the kind he had observed, was nothing more than the equivalent of "romantic fiction," warning that, "If the fiction ultimately fails to correspond with reality, it risks the breaking of hearts and the loss of its market."[44]

In defense of Charismatic Worship, in order to fulfill its purpose as "almost a sacrament" and as "a means of encountering God in his grace,"[45] there seems no way of avoiding language that is direct, immediate, ad-

---

36. Ibid., 71.
37. Ibid.
38. Ibid., 76.
39. Ibid., 79.
40. Ibid., 92.
41. Ibid., 96.
42. Ibid., 104.
43. Ibid., 100.
44. Ibid., 106.
45. Dyer, "Some Theological Trends," 37.

dressed to "You," the language, in other words of encounter. And, yes, it is anticipated by all those taking part that this will be a loving and intimate encounter. Perhaps, in fact, the quasi-eroticism of Charismatic Worship is not so much a thoughtless imbibing, or a "mirror of postmodern trends,"[46] but more of an antidote. The worshippers would doubtless share the conviction that the romantic intimacy which the world pursues can only truly find its answer in a unitive relationship with God: it is what we were created for and the worldly pursuit is a reflection of the desire in the creature for union with the Creator. The whole point of the Christian Beat groups of the 1960s was to offer precisely this antidote.

Theological and Grammatical Incompetence

As early as 1972, the newer worship music was criticized as "trivial," and therefore "a threat to the integrity of the Christian faith."[47] In defense of the early simplicity and freedom of Charismatic worship songs from "archaic or theological language,"[48] Scotland claimed, in 1995, that "their very simplicity was the key to their depth."[49] In 2003, Matt Redman stated that he was aiming for a balance between "revelation and response" and between "content and engagement."[50] Williams, writing in 2004, was able to claim that, in Charismatic Worship, "lyrics are becoming more theologically responsible."[51] However, in 2009, Goodiff noted the paradoxical reality that, while the most characteristic feature of the songs is their "Jesus-centeredness" yet, for all that, the Christology is woefully deficient,[52] amounting to little more than a "therapeutic Jesus."[53] The reasons for these deficiencies seem to be in the fact that none of the songwriters are theologically

---

46. Percy, "Sweet Rapture," 79.
47. Watkins, "Congregational Song," 87.
48. Scotland, *Charismatics and the Next Millennium*, 58.
49. Ibid., 57.
50. Redman, "Revelation and Response," in Redman, *Heart of Worship Files*, 11–14 and his "Content and Engagement," 154.
51. Williams, "Charismatic Worship," 149.
52. Goodiff, "'It's all About Jesus,'" 256. At least 59 percent of the songs he studied were about Jesus.
53. Goodiff, "'It's all About Jesus,'" 264.

trained.[54] Steven observes that the songwriters generally lack the theological acumen that Charles Wesley would have had.[55]

However, there may be more theology than we think there is in the musicality of the songs themselves. In its infancy is the study of the overall shape of the melodies and how they resolve. It could be that these melodies are speaking to us at a level far deeper and far more effectively than the words. Theology of the arts expert, Jeremy Begbie has begun to explore how elements in the music can "refer specifically to extra-musical phenomena."[56] While we sing, we may, for example, be picking up in the way a cadence resolves itself messages of home-coming or waiting.[57] This perhaps explains why many of the melodies use safe, predictable endings to musical phrases more than would be the norm in non-Christian pop music. The tone is soothing and reassuring.

However, there are issues with the words. A particular case in point is the bad grammar which pervades the lyrics of Hillsong and how, with such a vast international profile, no one seems to have checked them. Bebbington highlights only one of many similar examples where, for example, the phrase "The knowledge of your love as you live in me" is left to hang there as an unfinished sentence "without any following verb or complement."[58] He sees this as symptomatic of a decline in logocentricity such that we no longer care so much about words or the accuracy of their use.[59]

Commercialization

The origins of Charismatic Worship were grass roots and participative. In other words, it was the music of the people. As late as *Songs of Fellowship Volume 1*, compilations were made, in part at least, by actually visiting churches and finding out what was being sung, regardless of the songwriter.

---

54. A notable exception might be Ian White who earned a BD from Edinburgh. Though much loved by charismatics in the 1980s and 1990s, he remains a staunch Presbyterian, however.

55. Steven, "Charismatic Hymnody," 227. On this theme see also Harrison, "'There Must be More Than This'" 275–86, and Page, *And Now let's Move*.

56. Begbie, *Theology, Music and Time*, cited by Lim, "Methodologies of Musicking in Practical Theology," 312.

57. Lim, "Methodologies of Musicking," 312.

58. Bebbington, "Evangelicals and Public Worship," 19.

59. Ibid. "The word had lost part of its sacredness," he says.

Music that has come from the people deserves to be defined as true folk art, and its first emergence happened to coincide with a literal folk revival that was going on outside the Church.[60] Because of its folk character it naturally engendered a sense of participation, of the whole body of Christ, which, in turn, chimed with the desire to replicate 1 Corinthians 12–14 in the use of the spiritual gifts by the whole congregation.

More recently, Charismatic Worship music has been propagated via an increasingly complex web of organizations tending to privilege an ever-decreasing elite of worship song writers who saturate the market with a vast quantity of new songs every year. In smaller countries, the size of the market means that some parts of the market have a near monopoly on the industry.[61] One trend is clear, whether we look at Australia,[62] the US or the UK: Charismatic worship is no longer folk worship. "Music must have roots in the cultural inheritance of the people," says Watkins, who cites the Edwardian folk tune collector Ralph Vaughan Williams with approval, saying that:

> ... folk music is "an art which grows straight out of the needs of a people and for which a fitting and perfect form, albeit on a small scale, has been found by those people; an art which is indigenous and owes nothing to anything outside itself."[63]

Early Charismatic music matches the description of the popular American music that arose in the mid-twentieth century. It was:

> ... essentially unconcerned with artistic or philosophical idealism; a music based on established or newly diffused American raw materials; a "popular" music in the largest sense, broadly based, widespread, naive, and unselfconscious.[64]

---

60. Ward refers to the popularity of the bands Steeleye Span and Fairport Convention: Ward, *Selling Worship*, 183.

61. See Ward, *Selling Worship*, 183–95.

62. A number of studies of the Australian Pentecostal-Charismatic scene have recently appeared: Chant, *Heart of Fire*, Hughes, *The Pentecostals in Australia*, Clifton, *Pentecostal Churches in Transition*, Hughes, Fraser and Reid, *Australia's Religious Communities*, Hey, *Mega Churches: Origins, Ministry and Prospects*, Rose, Hughes and Bouma, *Re-Imagining Church*. I am indebted to a paper presented at the European Pentecostal Theological Association by Jon Newton, for this information: "Pentecostalism in Australia: Where's it at and Where's it Going?" 1 July 2015, Florence.

63. Watkins, "Congregational Song," 90, citing Williams, *National Music*, 22.

64. Watkins, "Congregational Song," 91, citing Hitchcock, *Music in the United States*, 44.

A Theological Shift?

Looking at the themes that are either emphasized or left out of Charismatic worship is quite illuminating, and may be indicative of the very nature Charismatic Christianity. A place to start is to revisit Bebbington's quadrilateral. As he says in countless different publications,[65] the four distinguishing marks of evangelicalism are: conversionism, activism, biblicism and crucicentrism. Ward notes the marked emphasis on conversionism and crucicentrism in *Youth Praise*, born of its evangelistic priorities.[66] The one, of course, relates to the other: it is cross-centered because conversion-orientated. The Charismatic worship idiom, by contrast, which had already fully taken shape less than a decade after the publication of *Youth Praise Book One*, had a very different purpose. Charismatic worship was designed to foster a direct encounter with God in the Spirit for people who were already well-established believers. Conversionism is therefore replaced by pneumaticentrism and crucicentrism replaced by ecclesiocentrism. The activism and Biblicism largely remains though takes different forms. Concerning the theological emphases in *Sound of Living Waters*, Ward is clear that,

> Central to this new emphasis was a fresh understanding of the church as a body gathered to receive the Spirit. . . . Thus the songs turn the gaze from what has happened to believers to what is now happening as the church gathers as a body to worship.[67]

In a similar vein, *Songs of Fellowship Volume 1* is almost devoid of any references to the historical Jesus,[68] with all the emphasis placed instead upon his heavenly reign as King of his Kingdom. Jesus is presented in "purely abstract terms"[69] with little reference to the atonement. Dyer similarly notes the priority of the resurrection and ascension over the suffering and death of Christ in all the Charismatic songbooks she surveyed from the 1980s, though this trend is slightly corrected in the 1990s.[70] She notes

---

65. E.g., *Evangelicalism in Modern Britain*, 2.

66. Ward, *Selling Worship*, 124–25. There is a correspondingly low emphasis on the Spirit (ibid., 126).

67. Ibid., 122.

68. Ibid., 136.

69. Ibid., 148.

70. Dyer, "Some Theological Trends," 40. See also Steven: "in charismatic hymnody the exalted Christ has almost completely overshadowed the gospel accounts of Jesus of

that, prior to 1990, less than 1 percent of songs are specifically about the death of Christ. Since 2000, this figure had risen to 4.4 percent.[71] She muses that perhaps the reason for this was that "in the early years of renewal the Holy Spirit needed to encourage the church in their identity in Christ in the heavenlies before they could reach out in true compassion to the suffering world."[72] The teaching that believers are seated with Christ in the heavenlies had been a particular emphasis in the teaching of Derek Prince and Selwyn Hughes during the seventies,[73] hence, perhaps, the emphasis on his heavenly reign.

Theologically then, the absence of the atonement is one of the most marked features of Charismatic worship when compared to its immediate predecessor, *Youth Praise*. The contrast is even more marked when it is compared to earlier evangelical hymnody. Here I will focus my statistics on the occurrences of the word "blood" in association with Jesus as a fairly failsafe (and easy-to-spot) indicator of the presence of atonement.[74] Keswick's *Hymns of Consecration and Faith*, for example is one of the most atonement dominated hymnals ever to have been produced, with almost 1 in 3 of its hymns referring to the blood of Jesus at least once. The *Salvation Army Song Book* is similar, with an average of 1 in 4 of its songs carrying at least one mention of the blood of Christ. In Ira Sankey's *Sacred Songs and Solos* 1 in 6 of its songs touch on the theme. The arguably more mainstream *Hymns Ancient and Modern* was first published in 1861. The ratio of hymns containing at least one reference to the blood in this hymnal is 1 in 8, and in its successor, the *English Hymnal* of 1906, the figure is down to 1 in 9. In these broad church hymnals, most of the references to the blood are restricted to the Eucharistic hymns, the hymns for the seasons of Lent and Passion tide and the section for "Mission Services." It is clear that the blood theme was generally much more important to worshippers with some level of holiness background or influence than to worshippers who were outside the sweep of holiness influence.

Classical Pentecostalism did not lose the crucicentric emphasis of the holiness movement. To the contrary, the classical Pentecostals seemed to be especially attached to atonement themes. Its pneumatological emphasis

---

Nazareth." *Worship in the Spirit*, 189.

71. Dyer, "Some Theological Trends," 41.
72. Ibid.
73. Ibid., 43.
74. A more detailed treatment of this theme is in my: *The Old Rugged Cross*, 125–28.

was added to but did not supplant the atonement emphasis. Emerging out of the Elim movement, in 1951, came the famous *Redemption Hymnal*. In this hymnbook of 800 hymns, there are 227 references to the blood of Christ, an average of well over one in every four hymns boasting at least one reference to the blood.

Returning now to *Sound of Living Waters* of 1974, while general atonement themes are by no means absent, including references to the slain Lamb and to Christ as crucified for us or as having died for us or paid the price for us—and the "Canticle of the Gift"[75] is an especially crucicentric song—1 in every 19 songs refers to the blood of Jesus.[76] In *Fresh Sounds* a mere 1 in 27 songs mention the blood of Jesus—just four songs in total. These include the old holiness classic, "There is Power in the Blood"[77]; a nascent spiritual warfare song, "Jesus is a-Drivin' Out Satan,"[78] which includes the line, "He gives us his blood and body/in his strength we must rest"; the hymn, "When I Survey"[79]; and "Come Follow Me Now,"[80] which includes a reference to drinking of Christ's blood.[81]

There has clearly been a very dramatic shift of emphasis. We are forced to potentially redefine Charismatic Christianity as something other than evangelical if Bebbington's quadrilateral holds. Charismatic Christianity's quadrilateral, if it has one at all, has dropped at least two of evangelicalism's most distinctive identity markers. Most significantly of all, it has dropped crucicentrism.

However, the picture would not be complete if we did not bring ourselves a little more up to date. In the 1980s, the more doctrinally loaded songs of Graham Kendrick brought back an emphasis on atonement. He was followed by Stuart Townend and Matt Redman in the 1990s and 2000s. Indeed, the first Soul Survivor songbook called itself *The Way of the Cross*.

---

75. No. 2
76. Nos. 17, 55, 63, 64, 68, 77, and 85.
77. No. 50.
78. No. 73.
79. No. 75.
80. No. 108.
81. "I share my body with the whole of the world; if you drink my blood, you will live evermore."

Redman sings that his "every road leads to the cross."[82] At the cross he is humbled by God's mercy and "broken inside."[83]

There has been a trend, albeit slight, away from prophetic progressivism in the direction a more traditional approach in both content and musicality. Two crucicentric songs in particular have been written by Townend and Getty that are, both musically and lyrically, in the style of a hymn: *In Christ Alone* and *Oh, to See the Dawn*. The language is theologically rich, emotive and atonement centered.

Conclusion

> ... the ideal course involves the eradication of the unknown, the choreography of "spontaneity," and the anticipation of all eventualities via textual calculus of the "real."[84]

Such is Catherine Pickstock's stark description of life in the secular city, the flattened out and wonder-less world of modernity which squints at the very idea of any transcendent reality. Because it believes so firmly that we came from nothing and are on our way to nowhere, secular modernity's outcomes ought to be entirely nihistic but because it cannot be that honest with itself, it is humanistic instead. And it is the urban world—an ever growing reality—that is where secularity most fully thrives. Yet this is also the very context where you are most likely to encounter full-hearted Charismatic worship. It is especially at home in the mega-church; though this was not always the case. The loss of the participative primitivism of the early days is something that perhaps ought to have been mourned more than it has been.

Harvey Cox has already noted the success of Pentecostalism, in the general sense of the word, in urban centers. He describes it as a "... communitarian counterforce within these bloated conurbations as they continue to swell and become progressively less liveable."[85] And this is the kind of counterbalance to urban life that Charismatic worship provides. It breaks apart Pickstock's descriptions of its pretensions to knowledge and its ambitions to control the spontaneous and codify the unpredictable.

---

82. Goodiff also notes his crucicentrism, a quality his songs seem to share with Martin Layzell: Goodiff, "'It's all About Jesus,'" 257–58 and 259–60.

83. Redman, *Jesus Christ (Once Again)*.

84. Pickstock, *After Writing*, 3.

85. Cox, *Fire from Heaven*, 15.

What about the loss of atonement-centeredness? We saw that there was one perfectly straightforward reason for this and that was a change in the audience for the songs. To a level that would not have been the case for any of the song and hymn collections that predate *Come Together*, the focus was on building Church. These new collections were entirely focused on meeting the needs of participants that were assumed to be very well established in the Christian faith but entirely new to life in the Spirit, and new to the life of the Spirit-filled Church.

However, it is equally clear that we search in vain for anywhere else in Charismatic faith where crucicentrism has been maintained. Conversionism too, can be hard to recognize, though we will look at Charismatic evangelism later in this book. In fact, it was this very absence of crucicentrism from Charismatic Christianity that led to me choosing theology as a career. I had been a Charismatic for four years when a spiritual crisis led to me finding some life-changing answers in the atonement—a subject that I had heard not a single sermon on. Nearly all the books available on the subject were of a rather academic nature. I found I had to rapidly acquire academic theological vocabulary just to be able to understand them fully. And once I learned the language of theologians it was not long before I become one. (I will let you guess what the subject of my PhD became.) I have concluded, and I am not being at all unkind in saying this, that Charismatics have little use for the atonement, little use, that is, for the conservative evangelical version of it. They have, however, shown signs of attraction to alternative models such as the patristic Ransom to Satan model, which has been reinvented by the Word of Faith teachers.[86] If Charismatic faith ever becomes truly crucicentric it will be in a way which evangelicalism would probably struggle to recognize.

---

86. See the ground-breaking studies of William Atkinson in "Nature of the Crucified Christ," 169–84; "A Theological Appraisal"; and Atkinson, *The Death of Jesus*.

3

Leading and Discipling

THE SHEPHERDING CONTROVERSY

Introduction

Of the five distinctive theological systems that Charismatics have innovated, the Shepherding Movement always looks like the odd one out. It lacks the claims made by the other four theologies to have gained some ability to control spiritual realities. It lays no claim on any overarching cosmology or metaphysic. It amounts to something rather prosaic: do as you're told and all will be well. Or is it that simple?

America: The Fort Lauderdale Five

The Fort Lauderdale Five were Ern Baxter, Derek Prince, Charles Simpson, Don Basham, and Bob Mumford. Simpson was the youngest (and is the only surviving) member of the team. Canadian Ern Baxter, a later addition to the team, was the oldest member. Each of the five had particular gifts, especially in the area of speaking and writing. The trigger for the welding of the Five together (at least the first four before Ern Baxter joined them) was the moral fall of the main editor of the magazine to which they were all regularly contributing: *New Wine*. The editor's moral fall happened in 1970, in response to which, the Four met in a hotel to discuss how to deal with the case in such a way as would protect the editor from media frenzy. As they talked they were bound together in a common concern. They noticed how when ministries are "submitted to no one, answerable to no one, they too often stumble."[1] They resolved from that moment they would all make themselves "accountable" to one another—using terminology and concepts that have now become commonplace. They all reported a palpable sense that the Holy Spirit did something in that meeting to bind them together in a mutually accountable collegiality. Christian Growth Ministries would eventually become the title adopted for their ministry.

Emphasis 1: Covenant Relationship

"Covenant relationship" soon became a central doctrine in their teaching: total, even lifelong, self-sacrificial commitment to leaders and fellow believers. The key thing that the Five thought was needed among the freewheeling House Churches was "discipleship through personal pastoral care,"[2] hence the use of "shepherd" language. Though revolutionary for its time, none of this was problematic in itself, but the way this pastoral care was structured was where the problems lay: "Down through the pyramid went the orders, it was alleged, while up the same pyramid went the tithes."[3] Male leadership, regular tithing, and submission of every aspect of life to the advice of a pastor was all assumed.

Emphasis 2: Cell Groups

The second main emphasis was the institution of cell groups led by lay pastors.[4] Here again, "cell group," a unit in which discipleship takes place, was new terminology. Cell groups provided the kind of intimate community for which people longed. And there was genuine concern over the well-being of Christians, especially those newly severed from the historic denominations: "People needed to belong, to be a part of something. There was a widespread cry for personal discipline; people hungered to get their lives

---

1. Moore, *Shepherding Movement*, 29.
2. Ibid., 1.
3. Hunter, "Shepherding Movement," in Burgess et al., *Dictionary Of Pentecostal And Charismatic Movements*, 784. The 2001 edition has an article written by S. D. Moore instead of the H. D. Hunter article.
4. Moore, *Shepherding Movement*, 2.

together."⁵ Bear in mind that, at least in America, many of the members of the House Churches were former hippies who had come to Christ through the Jesus Movement and had received no discipleship from anyone.

Britain: The Apostolic Networks

Emphasis 1: Restoring the New Testament church

There was a parallel development to the Fort Lauderdale Five going on in the UK within the House Church movement, later termed the Restorationist movement.⁶ It is also now known as the Apostolic Networks, because of the key belief in the present day office of apostle. And sometimes it is referred to as the British New Church Movement. The term "New Church" was coined by Gerald Coates as a way of recognizing that "House Church" had become no longer an accurate term to describe churches that had rapidly acquired their own premises. The title of Andrew Walker's history of the movement is well chosen: *Restoring the Kingdom*. There was a post-millennial eschatology undergirding the early years of the movement that filled the early leaders with a vision for the fully restored bride of Christ that would be ready for his return. Their reading of Ephesians 4 led them to firmly believe that this could not happen until all five of the Ephesians 4 ministries were restored to the Church, including apostles and prophets. There was much early debate over whether an apostle submits to a prophet or the other way around; though, there was a wide acceptance that accountability between all leaders was to be free-flowing, non-authoritarian, and non-denominational. All was based on voluntary relationships—real friendships rather than formal structural ties. The difficulty was with how these leaders then interacted with the rank and file of the growing numbers of congregations that were submitting to their apostolic oversight. Among one another, there was no hierarchy, only mutuality. Very often, in their churches, all was hierarchy.

---

5. Mumford, *Christianity Today*. Cited in Scotland, *Charismatics and the Next Millennium*, 95.

6. Walker, *Restoring the Kingdom* is the definitive history of the movement, though William Kay's *Apostolic Networks in Britain* supplies an analysis of the movement as it looks today.

Emphasis 2: Sanctification by Submission

The leadership and discipleship theology of the British aspect of the movement, while influenced by Ern Baxter's spellbinding platform speaking, seems to have had its own origin with the Argentine evangelist Juan Carlos Ortiz. He and a small entourage of other pastors from Buenos Aries visited the UK in 1972. Dave Tomlinson reminisces:

> "Jesus didn't commission us to go and make converts," they told us, "but to make disciples." . . . "It's simple," one of them explained. "All you have to do is get your people committed and submitted and then you can get on with the real business of discipleship."[7]

Ortiz himself, writes, in his highly influential book *Disciple*:

> I've heard Christians say very proudly, "I don't follow any man—I follow Christ." That sounds pious, but it's really a great mistake. It means the person wants to do his own will; he doesn't even realize what it means to follow Christ.[8]

> There is no formation without submission.[9]

> He commanded, and they did it. That is how disciples are formed.[10]

This kind of teaching provided an answer for church leaders whose religious authority was diminishing in a libertarian age.[11] Ortiz offered a compelling account of the innate rebellion of people even after professing faith in Christ. He made it very clear that it is possible to be a convert to Christianity but never to have made Jesus Lord; to be a Christian but not a true disciple. Submission to God's delegated authority was the key to stamping out this lingering rebellion in people so that they could grow, in

---

7. Tomlinson, "Shepherding: Care or Control?" in Osborn and Walker, *Harmful Religion*, 30.

8. Ortiz, *Disciple*, 101.

9. Ibid., 111.

10. Ibid.

11. In the UK, the 1960s saw an unprecedented undoing of Christian values in government legislation: the Obscene Publications Act of 1959; the legalization of Abortion and Homosexuality in 1967; the Theatre Act of 1968. Added to this was the advent of the contraceptive pill in 1965. These factors all contributed to the removal of restraint in society and, because it was happening at such a high level, caused religious leaders to feel powerless.

the words of Ephesians 4, into "the measure of the stature of the fullness of Christ"(Eph 4:13).

Watchman Nee was also highly influential, and, with the title of one of his books, appears to have coined the term "spiritual authority," a term still used in some Charismatic circles:

> To reject delegated authority is an affront to God.[12]

> Whether the one in authority is right or wrong does not concern us since he has to be responsible directly to God.[13]

Various horror stories soon began to emerge,[14] especially from Bryn Jones' Covenant Ministries. People were required to submit their holiday plans, romantic intentions, financial plans—everything, to their shepherd. Members of Noel Stanton's *Jesus Army* were not even free to leave. During the 1980s, teaching on authority in British charismatic churches chimed with the tough right-wing Thatcherism of the day and enjoyed a strong following among the middle class businessmen and their families that formed the bulk of most charismatic congregations. Where controversy existed, it was minor compared to the storm that soon enveloped the American scene.

What Became of the Shepherding Movement?

The initial success of the movement in America was striking. *New Wine Magazine,* the voice of Christian Growth Ministries, soon reached a circulation of 130,000. Over the course of 1970–72, submission ideas were freely articulated through this magazine seemingly with no thought to how these might be abused by the power-hungry. In March 1973 the first Shepherds conference attracted 450 leaders. In June 1974 the second Shepherds conference attracted 1,700 delegates. This was followed in 1975 by the National Men's Shepherds Conference, which drew 4,700. Over the course of 1974–75 entire national networks of churches and prayer groups began to submit themselves to the Five. An offer was extended to the entire British House Church Movement at this time, proposing Ern Baxter as the key

---

12. Nee, *Spiritual Authority*, 71.
13. Ibid.
14. There are some in Scotland, *Charismatics and the Next Millennium*, 93–94. See also, Johnson and Van Vonderen, *Subtle Power of Spiritual Abuse*, 17–19, 21–22.

overseer of this part of the empire, but the offer was refused. The Five constantly stressed the importance of commitment, loyalty, and servanthood.

The controversy began in 1975. In that year, Christian Growth Ministries was denounced on air by Pat Robertson for its "cultic excesses." Demos Shakarian followed suit by forbidding the Five access to Full Gospel Business Men's Fellowship meetings. They were publicly denounced by all three of the most celebrated leaders of the Charismatic movement of the time: Kathryn Kuhlman, Dennis Bennett, and David DuPlessis. The Five were widely accused of control and the overuse of authority. The movement soon became "the most divisive issue since the rise of the Charismatic Renewal in the historic churches."[15] Even the *New York Times* ran an article on it.[16]

In March 1976, at the Charismatic Leaders Conference, the Five offered a mild apology for any problems their teachings had caused.[17] However, there lingered an underlying (and certainly unjustified) suspicion that the Five were trying to take over the whole Charismatic movement in America.

Between 1978 and 1980, Bob Mumford and Charles Simpson were spending a lot of time travelling around the churches trying to deal with abuses. Internal conflicts between the Five led to their separation in 1980. In December 1986, the last issue of *New Wine* appeared.[18] In 1989, Don Basham died. In 1993, Ern Baxter died. In 2003, Derek Prince died, having already renounced the movement in 1984. Only Simpson continues today, pastoring Covenant Church, Mobile, Alabama.[19]

S. David Moore, the only academic authority on the Shepherding Movement, assesses it quite positively as the movement that blazed the trail for the current ecclesiocentrism that has become so prevalent and which overtly speaks the language of discipleship and accountability that the Five pioneered.[20] What seems clear is that the movement was primarily part of a wider reaction in the 70s against the secular liberalization of the 60s.

---

15. McDonnell, "Seven Documents on the Discipleship Question," in McDonnell, *Presence, Power, Praise*, 116.

16. Moore, *Shepherding Movement*, 3.

17. See full report in Moore, *Shepherding Movement*, 194.

18. Moore chooses this as the date for the end of the movement (*Shepherding Movement*, 14).

19. See his book, *The Challenge to Care*, which serves as an apologetic for the movement. On pp. 79–84 he gives a very brief history of the controversy from his own perspective.

20. E.g., Moore, *Shepherding Movement*, 190.

The libertarianism of the 60s did not in fact reflect the values of America's "silent majority." Nixon, with his election in 1968, began to restore the fortunes of right wing, conservative America: the America of the Bible Belt. The Charismatic Renewal had also helped to revitalize conservative Christianity. The election of born again Jimmy Carter in 1976 set the seal on this religious-right wing triumph. The Fort Lauderdale Five were part of this bouncing back of the religious right as they attempted, at the level of individual pastoral care, to deal with the ravages of America's new liberalism. The pyramid structures allowed the teachings of the Five to penetrate effectively all the way down to the individual Christian struggling to refuse the temptations of a newly liberalized popular culture.

As we turn to the longer term outcomes in Britain, the story is not one of a sudden coming and going, but a gradual evolution. The very strong Brethren influence that affected the ecclesiology of the British movement prevented leaders from becoming excessive.

The high octane postmillennial expectation of a restored New Testament church overseen by present-day apostles heralding the return of Christ has now faded. And with the transition to a new generation of leaders who are imbued with a more *laissez faire* postmodern approach to authority, the doctrine that submission to spiritual authority is the key to growth in discipleship, does not seem set to survive the succession process that most of the Apostolic Networks are now going through.

Case Study: Covenant Ministries Re-invents Itself

A visit to the website of what is now called Life Church, Bradford, reveals absolutely nothing of this church's past.[21] There is no indication that this church is the same church that, under the leadership of fiery Welsh preacher, Bryn Jones, was to be the most notorious of all for its shepherding excesses, so complete and so successful has been its re-invention. In fairness, it does appear that Jones received unfair criticisms. William Kay, in writing his history of Covenent Ministries, seems convinced that Jones had no designs on adopting any kind of popish role.[22] If anything, it appears to have been Bryn's brother Keri that was the more controlling of the two. The few disenchanted couples who received much publicity were all it took

---

21. http://www.lifechurchhome.com/welcome/.
22. Kay, *Apostolic Networks in Britain*, 55.

to tarnish his reputation, despite the six hundred or so congregants that remained loyal to his leadership.

Bryn Jones's baby was Covenant Ministries International, a Restoration ministry that saw huge success between the founding of the main church at Church House in Bradford in 1976 and 1989 when new headquarters was opened near Coventry.[23] This ministry earned Jones his place as, "along with Arthur Wallis . . . the single most influential architect of Restorationism in Britain."[24] The Dales and Downs Bible Weeks that he pioneered were the forerunners of Stoneleigh, Spring Harvest, New Wine, and Soul Survivor. As early as 1984, Bryn Jones's ability to release other apostolic ministries that he had founded was shown by his releasing of Terry Virgo to found his own ministry in the South East: New Frontiers International in Brighton. While this releasing of protégés would continue—sometimes to the chagrin of Keri—by the early 1990s, Covenant Ministries International was becoming a centralized bureaucracy that was increasingly distant from both elders and congregations (which numbered possibly as many as seventy churches by his time). The apostles at the top of the organization were not tolerant of anyone voicing misgivings, and there was no genuine peer accountability.[25] There was also an inability to engage with the wider Church despite aspirations to unite the whole Body of Christ in a new restored New Testament wineskin freed from denominational trappings.[26]

In 1990, Jones handed the congregation in Bradford to Paul Scanlon while he built up a new multi-purpose facility in Coventry. By 1997, Scanlon became one of three key men that Bryn Jones formally recognized and released as apostles. These younger leaders, whom Jones had fathered, were not proving as loyal as he had hoped. Within a year, Scanlon had gone independent and was beginning a process referred to as the "crossing over." In new premises, he pioneered the now world famous megachurch, Abundant Life Ministries, home to pop idol Gareth Gates. Bryn Jones died in 2003,[27] and Scanlon soon jettisoned titles such as "apostle," referring to himself as

---

23. See Robertson, "Evaluative History," 78.

24. Hewitt, *Doing a New Thing*, 34.

25. Robertson notes an occasion when there was a parting of the ways with a leader over the matter of head coverings for women: Robertson, "An Evaluative History of Covenant Ministries," 87. Bryn latterly became open to jettisoning the head coverings, while Keri would not back down: Robertson, "Evaluative History," 84.

26. Ibid., 85.

27. There is a website dedicated to his memory and influence: http://www.theradicalchurch.com/#/bryn-jones/life-death.

"Senior Pastor." By 2007 this congregation numbered 2,500 and had its own TV station and schools of leadership and music. In 2013, it was handed on to Steve and Charlotte Gambill, with Scanlon taking a lower level of leadership. It presently numbers about 3000 members.

Conclusion

In 1995 William Cavanaugh wrote one of the most penetrating critiques of secular modernity ever written. There is an interesting refrain which emerges:

> What is left to the Church is increasingly the purely interior government of the souls of its members; their bodies are handed over to the secular authorities. . . . The concept of religion being born here is one of domesticated belief systems which are, insofar as it is possible, to be manipulated by the sovereign for the benefit of the State. Religion is no longer a matter of certain bodily practices within the Body of Christ, but is limited to the realm of the 'soul' and the body is handed over to the State . . . The modern Church thus splits the body from the soul and purchases freedom of religion by handing the body over to the State[28]

The result of secular modernity's "persistent project to neutralize the public sphere,"[29] is that the forces of public discipline lie with the state, a state which provides for and lays absolute claim to everyone's physical existence: their bodies, but which keeps religion in a "punishment corner of privatization,"[30] where it has been more or less ever since the end of the Wars of Religion in 1648. This was when the very terms "religious" and "secular" were invented.[31]

An obvious result of this marginalization process was a gradual loss of disciplinary authority on the part of the leaderships of churches. Their authority was profoundly relativized. Nevertheless, such a limitation on authority was tolerable until the moral liberalism of the surrounding culture reached a certain tipping point, as it did in the 1960s. As we saw, the advent of what seem to us to be authoritarian styles of leadership was only one part

---

28. Cavanaugh, "Fire Strong Enough," 399, 405, 415.
29. Smith, *Introducing Radical Orthodoxy*, 32.
30. Cavanaugh, "Fire Strong Enough," 410.
31. It is interesting to note that Charismatics are in the habit of refusing to describe themselves as "religious." They hate the designation and all its associations.

of a wider reaction on the part of the whole of conservative America against the liberalism of the all-too influential minority. In such a situation a crisis of discipleship develops in which the quest for discipleship, already hopelessly privatized and intellectualized by the influence of secular modernity, is more seriously challenged by liberalized morals. During the sixties and seventies, the state tended to endorse the growing laxity. And the state, as Cavanaugh described, laid total claim to everyone's bodies. This state was now legalizing and endorsing lifestyles in which what one could do with one's body was heading towards new norms. It was next to impossible for leaders of churches to tell people that they should not, in fact, be doing those things with their bodies. The Church had no authority.

While no one would deny the seriousness of the abuses, a case can be made for the Shepherding movement to be identified as a flawed attempt to make precisely the kind of response to the situation that Cavanaugh proposed. He advocated that the "discipline" of the state—its claim over our bodies—should be opposed by a "counter-discipline"[32] and that this counter-discipline was best termed "discipleship." Since the days of the Shepherding movement, interest in discipleship has grown considerably. The very best of these efforts avoid creating the kind of aura around Christian leaders that the Shepherding movement did. They avoid doing what seemed the obvious step to take in the sixties and seventies: bolster the religious authority of church leaders. Instead of this counter-discipline, there is the counter-discipline of holism to counteract the compartmentalism that the secular world imposes. "There is no compartmentalization of the faith," says one discipleship advocate, "no realm, no sphere, no business, no politic in which the lordship of Christ will be excluded. We either make him Lord of all lords, or we deny him as Lord of any."[33] Mark Greene and Neil Hudson of the London Institute for Contemporary Christianity have a name for this: it is called "whole-life discipleship."[34] In this model, instead of having to submit to the spiritual authority of an apostle, church members are empowered to resist the sacred-secular divide and equipped to reach out to their own particular front-lines of mission in their work, education, and home life.

---

32. Cavanaugh, "Fire Strong Enough," 414–15.

33. Camp, *Mere Discipleship*, 19.

34. Greene, *Great Divide*; Cotterell and Hudson, *Leading a Whole-Life Disciplemaking Church*; Hudson, *Imagine Church*.

So here we have a Charismatic innovation that basically got its approach wrong but was right to get intentional about discipleship. It also drew attention to the role of "apostles" in contemporary church life though such a subject seems slightly beyond the scope of this book.[35]

---

35. For a thorough analysis, see McNair Scot, *Apostles Today*.

4

Praying Effectively

The Word of Faith Doctrine

You will notice that this chapter is somewhat thicker with references to the primary literature than other chapters. This is partly because of the sheer abundance of books and booklets that have poured from the pens of the practitioners of Word of Faith. I have been happy to trawl through whatever I could lay my hands on. And partly, the abundant and careful referencing of their written works is designed to be an antidote to the journalistic exposés that have tended to sieze upon heat-of-the-moment phrases taken from audio recordings.

A Brief History

Just as the Shepherding controversy was taking place, an alternative, more permissive Charismatic theology was emerging to replace or complement it: the Word of Faith or Positive Confession movement. Its famous maxim was: "You can have what you say," based on Mark 11:23, and sometimes parodied as "name it and claim it," or, "blab it and grab it." The flipside of this was that negative confessions had an equal and opposite power.

Kenneth Hagin is the recognized father of the movement but his teachings were taken to further extremes by such luminaries as Kenneth Copeland, who taught that the universe was governed by laws that the force of faith can manipulate; the great Earl Paulk, who taught that we are little gods; and the remarkable Charles Capps, who taught that everything is controlled by the power of human speech. Others included Fredrick Price, Jerry Savelle, Jesse Duplantis, Creflo Dollar, Lester Sumrall, John Avanzini, T. D. Jakes, and the very welcome female voice of Joyce Meyer, many of whom are still very active in ministry today. The main doctrines which they nearly all share are such things as: Revelation Knowledge, a certain concept of Faith which we will explore, Healing, and Prosperity. Most of the key ideas originate not with Hagin but with E. W. Kenyon (1867–1948).

The Faith controversy began in 1978. The Word of Faith movement was denounced by Charles Farah and Gordon Fee, deconstructed later by Dan McConnell, and written off as heresy by Hank Hanegraaff and others. In 1980 Larry Parker's *We Let Our Son Die* recounted the story of how, under the encouragement of a Word of Faith-influenced ladies prayer group, the Parkers refused their diabetic son insulin as an act of faith, resulting in his death and the prosecution of both parents. Ostracism by the wider evangelical community tends to have bred a persecution complex that further reinforces the Faith message. The original advocates of the Faith message do not appear to have changed their views at all, despite the controversy; although, Joyce Meyer's version of Word of Faith doctrine seems to represent an entirely new and much more moderate reinvention of it.

Some able critiques were offered by Dan McConnell[1] and others in the late eighties, though there have also been some able defenses offered by Joe McIntyre,[2] William DeArteaga,[3] and, most recently, Paul King.[4] Less favorable scholarly critiques have also continued to appear, especially in response to the prevalence of the prosperity message in Black churches and in sub-Saharan Africa.[5]

Faith doctrines have been propagated far and wide by TV, tapes and CDs, magazines, a profusion of books and pamphlets, and lately via the internet, to the point where Faith concepts are discernable in many churches not directly related to the movement. The vocabulary and spirituality of the Faith message has now penetrated a great deal of Christian ministry. People

---

1. McConnell, *A Different Gospel*.
2. McIntyre, *E. W. Kenyon and His Message of Faith*.
3. DeArteaga, *Quenching the Spirit*.
4. King, *Only Believe*.
5. Williams, "Heresy of Prosperity Teaching," 33–44; Perriman, *Faith, Health and Prosperity*; Harrison, *Righteous Riches*; Ayegboyin, "Rethinking of Prosperity Teaching," 70–86; Mitchem, *Name it and Claim it*; Wright, "Lausanne Theology Working Group Statement," 99–102.

no longer simply "pray"; they "speak it into being"; they "speak healing" to bodies; they "speak" to mountains and "declare victory."

A Brief Summary of "Faith"

At the heart of the movement is a belief about gaining cosmic control of the universe via the power of creative spoken words. The evidence that such control has been gained is a release of physical and material blessings. Arising out of a believer's born again nature comes faith. Out of faith comes the power to change reality by the use of positive confession. In effect, just as God creates by his spoken word, so, his children also create things by their spoken words. "Faith" for Kenyon, the originator of Hagin's ideas, may be described as the activation of an inner divine life[6] with regards to specific needs. According to Kenyon, it is the exercising of an inner divinity by which all things are possible:

> Who is in you? It is God! Then to the God who is in you, all things are possible. If you give that God within you liberty, let Him loose in you, you become limitless in your realm.[7]

Like Kenyon, Hagin states repeatedly that God is a "Faith God" who imparts this same Faith to believers.

> God believed that what He said would come to pass. He spoke the Word, and there was an earth. . . . He said it and it was so! That is the God-kind of faith. . . . Jesus demonstrated the God-kind of faith to His disciples, and then he told them that they, too, had that kind of faith.[8]

Hagin also developed the idea, not only of the imperative of positive confessions, but also of the perils of a negative, or "double" confession:

> Remember, your confession of Satan's ability to keep you from success gives him dominion over you. . . . You see, when you confess your doubts, fears, weakness, and disease, you are openly confessing that God's Word is not true.[9]

---

6. It is the "creative ability" in humans: Kenyon, *Hidden Man*, 73.
7. Kenyon, *In His Presence*, 115.
8. Hagin, *New Thresholds of Faith*, 81.
9. Hagin, *How to Turn Your Faith Loose*, 28.

Hagin shared with Kenyon his view of regeneration as involving an implantation of God's nature, which Hagin described as God's *Zoe*: "*Zoe*, then, means eternal life, or God's life. This new kind of life is God's nature. It produces certain changes in man."[10]

On the basis of Mark 11:23 and Kenyon's writings, Hagin seems to have been convinced that spoken words have the power to create reality.[11] Copeland then developed this belief in words as the means of releasing the God-Kind of Faith, seeing Faith as the operator of cosmic law. Copeland affirmed, along with Hagin, that Faith can be obstructed by negative confessions. Charles Capps then went further still, deducing that words are the cause of everything in the universe. By harnessing the power of words, therefore, anything is possible in this universe, whether good or bad, since words create reality.

The difficulties begin when reasons have to be found as to why the creative force of Faith does not always succeed in creating anything. The need to confess and keep on confessing, as well as the need to take into account the opposing forces of fear and unbelief, with their attendant negative confessions, have all proven popular in this regard.

New Thought Philosophy and Faith

The McConnell Thesis

A link between the nineteenth-century metaphysical cults and the Faith movement, via the writings of nineteenth-century preacher E. W. Kenyon, has been notoriously difficult to prove.[12] E. W. Kenyon was originally a

---

10. Hagin, *Zoe: The God-Kind of Life*, 9. Cf. 14, 16, 18, 19, 21.

11. "Faith's confessions create reality." Hagin, *How to Turn Your Faith Loose*, 23.

12. McConnell concedes: "we do not have any *written* confession by Kenyon which admits to having formed his theology from cultic sources." McConnell, *Different Gospel*, 25 (italics original). Some prefer to cite some contemporary influence such as the New Age movement: Smail, Walker, and Wright, "'Revelation Knowledge' and Knowledge of Revelation," in Smail, Walker, and Wright, *Charismatic Renewal*, 135–36. Sarles believes he can point to the Positive Thinking and Positive Mental Attitude teachings of Norman Vincent Peale and Robert Schuller as direct influences upon the Faith movement: Sarles, "Theological Evaluation," 329–30, as does Williams, "Prosperity Teaching," 197–208. Da Silva cites both the New Age movement and the positive thinking advocates: Da Silva, "'Theology of Success' Movement," 91. Hunt and McMahon see the New Age as happening outside the Church. Their concern is with the influence today of New Thought within the Church: Hunt and McMahon, *Seduction of Christianity*, 151. All of these writers may

Methodist, then lost his faith for a time and attended Emerson School of Oratory[13] because of an ambition to become an actor. He then returned to his faith under the preaching of A. J. Gordon and went on to become a Baptist minister.[14] The contention is that, while attending Emerson School of Oratory and having lost his Christian faith for a time, he fell under spell of the cult that then dominated the college: New Thought philosophy. Indeed, a fellow student at the time was Ralph Waldo Trine himself. This is thought to best explain the rather unusual elements that then turn up in Kenyon's writings after he had returned to his faith. And it seems to have been these aspects of Kenyon's thought that would later be especially attractive to Kenneth Hagin, prompting him to develop his distinctive, "You can have what you say" mantra.

New Thought strikes its roots into Transcendentalism.[15] The Transcendentalists of New England were idealists inspired by German philosophy that had passed through the filters of Romantic writers such as Samuel Coleridge and Thomas Carlyle. According to the Transcendentalists humans possessed a higher faculty of reason, way beyond Lokean sense interpretation, that they called "intuition" or even "faith."[16] By this faculty, this faith, this "spiritual intimation,"[17] humans were capable of direct encounter with God. Many were from Christian backgrounds but had become Unitarians in their pursuit of "nondogmatic experimentalism."[18] The heart of the Transcendentalist idea, according to Buell, was "the idea of a divinity latent within each person, whose ordinarily underactivated potential is not to be

---

be able to point out similarities with contemporary spiritualities but evidence of any dependence on them is lacking. The search for an historical influence at the movement's point of inception, though certainly problematic, seems more promising.

13. Academic year: 1892–93.

14. See the biographical details supplied by Lie, "E. W. Kenyon," 6–15. Also Lie, "E. W. Kenyon" *Journal of the European Pentecostal Theological Association*, 71–86.

15. For good introductions to this immensely influential movement see: Frothingham, *Transcendentalism in New England*, 1; Buell, *American Transcendentalists*, xxii–xxv, Gura, *American Transcendentalism*, 53–68.

16. Friedrich Jacobi (1743–1819) seems to have been the first to describe it in this way. In J. D. Morell's *An Historical and Critical View of the Speculative Philosophy of Europe in the Nineteenth Century* of 1841, "faith" was explained to American readers in this way: "Just as sensation gives us immediate knowledge of the world, so there is an inward sense—a rational intuition—a spiritual faculty—by which we have a direct and immediate revelation of supersensual things." Cited in Gura, *American Transcendendalism*, 54.

17. Ibid.

18. Buell, *American Transcendentalists*, xviii.

reasoned into being so much as ignited."[19] Perhaps not surprisingly, one of the principal doctrines of the New England Transcendentalists was "the supremacy of mind over matter."[20] They were reacting, as all Romantics were at the time, to the "cool rationality of Enlightenment materialism and deism."[21]

New Thought applied Transcendentalist beliefs in practical terms towards the procurement of health, wealth, and happiness. The following are the words of P. P. Quimby, founder of New Thought philosophy, and, via his influence on Mary Baker Eddy, effectively the founder of Christian Science:

> Now when people are educated to understand that *what they believe they will create,* they will cease believing what the medical men say, and try to account for their feelings in a more rational way.[22]

Quimby's main concern was with healing, yet it was clear that his beliefs about the powerful effects of thinking positively had much wider ramifications. Quimby had already described his beliefs as the "Science of Life"[23] and the "Science of Happiness."[24] The implications of his message were soon noticed. Warren F. Evans, Mary Baker Eddy, Annetta G. Seabury, and Julius A. Dresser were the first to popularize the beliefs of Quimby.[25] As a result, a holistic philosophy of life emerged that perceived the secret not only of bodily healing, but also of prosperity and well-being of every kind was to exclude all negative thoughts and maintain a positive outlook on life.[26] Others, taking their cue from Warren F. Evans, then took Quimby's beliefs a stage further and began to include the idea of positive verbal affirmations.[27] These ideas became highly influential.[28]

---

19. Ibid., xxiii.
20. Braden, *Spirits in Rebellion*, 28–9.
21. Anderson, "Idealism in American Thought," 24.
22. Dresser, *Quimby Manuscripts*, 263 (italics original).
23. Ibid., 241.
24. Ibid., 253.
25. Braden, *Spirits in Rebellion*, 89.
26. Neuman, "Cultic Origins," 40.
27. Ibid., 40–41. See also Braden, *Spirits in Rebellion*, 122–23.
28. Toward the end of the nineteenth century, New Thought ideas seem to have become quite pervasive. Ralph Waldo Trine comments to a friend: "How beautiful if Emerson, the illumined one so far in advance of his time, who labored so faithfully and so fearlessly to bring about these very conditions, how beautiful if he were here with us

Henry Wood developed the teaching of Evans on positive affirmations, suggesting various affirmative statements to speak out in groups, to place on the walls or to meditate on in solitude. Here is a sample of some:

> The Word which is within, I speak to externals ... I am a sculptor, and thinking is my chisel ... I rule my bodily conditions. ... I bury all negation, weakness, and fear. I enthrone and embody the positive, living truth. ... I am strong in the Lord. ... I am full of faith. ... I heal and am healed ... I am building the world in which I must live ...[29]

Like the Transcendentalists, New Thought writers were fond of the word, "faith," but in the way they use this term, faith becomes something entirely subjective. It is no longer necessary that there be a God to have faith in, simply that there be "faith." It is seen in Wood as a self-contained creative power.[30] For Ralph Waldo Trine, faith was "the operation of the *thought forces* in the form of an earnest desire, coupled with the expectation as to its fulfilment."[31] In Quimby, the very same idea is given the term "Mind," to which he gives the new meaning, "matter held in solution."[32] Mind can materialize its own reality.

McIntyre argues strenuously throughout his book that it was the Faith Cure advocates such as Charles Cullis, A. B. Simpson, and A. J. Gordon, and later, John Alexander Dowie and Carrie Judd-Montgomery that were "documentably" Kenyon's "mentors" rather than Charles Emerson, Ralph Waldo Trine, or anyone else of New Thought inclinations.[33] However, the documentation that McIntyre is able to cite in support of these evangelical

---

today to witness it all! How he would rejoice!" Trine, *In Tune with The Infinite* (original, 1897), 17.

29. Wood, *New Thought Simplified*, 53–60.

30. "Faith, far from being mere emotion, is really concentrated spiritual and psychical momentum, and this momentum has tremendous potential force." Wood, *New Thought Simplified*, 20.

31. Trine, *In Tine with the Infinite*, 19 (italics his).

32. "Then what is it that is not Wisdom, God, or spirit, and not matter and yet can be changed? It is matter held in solution called Mind, which the power of Wisdom can condense into a solid so dense as to become the substance called "matter." Assume this theory and you can see how man can become sick and get well by a change of Mind." Dresser, *Quimby Manuscripts*, 234. Hanegraaff may well have been right in his observation that, "... the distinction between the 'mind' of metaphysics and the 'faith' of Faith theology is little more than cosmetic." Hanegraaff, *Christianity in Crisis*, 30.

33. McIntyre, *E. W. Kenyon and His Message of Faith*, 46, 242, 245–64, cf.19.

influences on Kenyon is somewhat meagre.³⁴ Moreover, there are comments made by those who knew Kenyon before his death in 1948 that seem to quite convincingly demonstrate the influence of the metaphysical cults on his thought. One of Kenyon's closest former acquaintances mused: "I have come to realize that E. W. Kenyon has simply 'baptized' many concepts from Christian Science. In so doing, he became a source for a form of 'Pentecostal Christian Science.'"³⁵ In a taped interview, Ern Baxter also spoke of how Kenyon read Mary Baker Eddy's *Science and Health with Key to the Scriptures* with approval. Baxter goes on to say that "he was well-read in metaphysics, in the writings of Ralph Waldo Emerson and in New England Transcendentalism."³⁶ DeArteaga and Perriman believe that the Faith Cure movement and New Thought actually exchanged ideas and that Kenyon was a prime example of that confluence of ideas and terminology.³⁷ America, after all, was in the throes of a reaction against Enlightenment materialism in both its Christian and non-Christian guises, which, according to Menzies, also provided the conditions for Pentecostalism to arise.³⁸ In the wake of the Civil War, widespread commercial as well as philosophic materialism had swept through the devastated country in an all-out pursuit of power and plenty. The Church had been increasingly accommodating itself to the wealthy middle classes and swelling as a result.³⁹ All of this

---

34. In his book, I found six documented instances of a possible relationship between Kenyon and the Holiness and Faith-Cure teachers: A sermon by A. T. Pierson about having resurrected life like Christ's made a significant impact upon him; Kenyon once spoke in praise of Charles Cullis and of John Alexander Dowie; Kenyon once cited a certain F. L. House; Kenyon also recorded the influence of a little known preacher, John Norvell with regards to positive confession; and an advert for A. B. Simpson's church, The Interdenominational Gospel Tabernacle, features a billing of Kenyon as the guest speaker, McIntyre, *E. W. Kenyon and His Message of Faith*, 10, 67, 68, 227, 259, 273.

35. McConnell, *A Different Gospel*, 15, citing John Kenningham, unpublished written statement, Portland, Oregon, July 8, 1986.

36. McConnell, *A Different Gospel*, 184.

37. "Kenyon's system of faith idealism was a major codification of the idealist elements already present in both the Faith-Cure and Metaphysical movements." DeArteaga, *Quenching the Spirit*, 212. Also: Perriman, *Faith, Health and Prosperity*, 76. Similarly, A. J. Gordon was apparently influenced by Mary Baker Eddy: Dayton, *Theological Roots of Pentecostalism*, 122. See also Cunningham's discussion: Cunningham, "From Holiness to Healing," 512.

38. "In retrospect, the quest for Christian holiness seems to have been a popular expression of the strivings which on a more sophisticated level produced the transcendentalist revolt of Emerson and Thoreau." Menzies, *Anointed to Serve*, 24.

39. Anderson, *Vision of the Disinherited*, 29–30. Nichol cites Clifton Olmstead:

produced a cultural Christianity largely devoid of any supernatural power. Indeed any signs of "enthusiasm" or excess in revival meetings were increasingly suppressed.[40] The Church was mostly cessationist in outlook.[41]

The metaphysical cults, by contrast, were gaining large numbers of disillusioned Christians owing to the tangible results they were able to show for their beliefs. This was especially the case in the realm of healing. Within the Church, both the Faith Cure preachers and E. W. Kenyon had the common aim of offering a viable Christian alternative to the metaphysical cults. "We cannot ignore the amazing growth," says Kenyon, "of Christian Science, Unity, New Thought, and Spiritism. The people who are flocking to them are not the ignorant masses, but the most cultured and wealthy of the land, and their strongest appeal is the supernatural element of their so-called religion."[42]

Among the Faith Cure teachers there can certainly be found the great emphasis on faith as total confidence in the Word of God that would later become one of the distinguishing marks of Faith teaching.[43] This emphasis on the kind of faith that actually gets results can be traced as far back as Charles Finney (1792–1875).[44] However, what was to become the unique

---

"Never before in this country's history . . . had the Church been stronger in membership and weaker in spiritual soundness." Nichol, *Pentecostalism*, 25.

40. Anderson, *Vision of the Disinherited*, 38.

41. A. J. Gordon's book, *The Ministry of Healing*, of 1882, was largely written to counteract this: Graf, *Healing: The Three Great Classics*, 121–271. See DeArteaga, *Quenching the Spirit*, 118–26 for further documentation of the Faith Cure clash with cessationism. Also, Cunningham, "From Holiness to Healing," 512.

42. Kenyon, *The Wonderful Name of Jesus*, 110.

43. McIntyre also brings to light some teaching by A. B. Simpson on faith's relationship to confession in his 1892 book, *In Heavenly Places*, McIntyre, *E. W. Kenyon and His Message of Faith*, 65–66. Simpson stressed, however, that faith had to be based on what God Himself has actually said: "Therefore, whenever faith can clearly know that God has spoken, all it has to do is lay the whole responsibility on Him and go forward." Simpson, *Standing on Faith*, 23. Similarly, A. J. Gordon gives place to the sovereignty of God in his understanding of healing: "It is as true here as in any other field that God acts sovereignly and according to His own determinate counsel. He sees it best to recover one person at the instance of His people's prayers, and He may see it best to withhold such recovery for the time from another." Gordon Graf (ed), *Healing: The Three Great Classics*, 248. Carrie Judd-Montgomery's doctrine of faith included the important element of dependence upon God to bring to realization what faith has requested: "Our part is simply to reckon our prayer as answered, and God's part is to *make faith's reckonings real*." "Faith's Reckonings," 2–3, cited by Dayton, *Theological Roots of Pentecostalism*, 126.

44. Perriman, *Faith, Health and Prosperity*, 59, Goff, "Faith That Claims," 18–19 and Farah, "Critical Analysis," 5.

element in Faith teaching, that of faith being the power to autonomously speak things into being, is not found in Christian writings in any developed form until Kenyon.[45] What is found in Kenyon is a doctrine of faith and confession that goes significantly beyond anything that had been taught within any of the Christian traditions of the time.

The Word of Faith Teachers: Some Key Examples

Kenneth Hagin

Kenneth E. Hagin is sometimes referred to as "Daddy Hagin" on account of his place in history as founder of the Faith movement. However, the significance of Kenyon's thought to Hagin is undeniable. McConnell has placed beyond doubt the word-for-word, paragraph-for paragraph and idea-for-idea plagiarism of Kenyon's books that Kenneth Hagin has been repeatedly guilty of. McConnell has convincingly shown that all of Hagin's major ideas came from the works of E. W. Kenyon.[46]

Theologically, Hagin was not an innovator and was actually a good deal more conservative than Kenyon. His teaching was filled with stories and much of what he taught was quite unremarkable. Hagin takes Kenyon's concept of faith and anchors it more firmly into the everyday needs of people. The main need that he focuses on is healing.[47] This is not surprising, considering his own testimony of healing as a sixteen-year-old boy, as well as his involvement with the post-World War II healing evangelists. He also draws out more of the implications of this particular concept of faith with regards to financial needs.[48] Like Kenyon, Hagin states repeatedly that God is a Faith God who imparts this same Faith to believers:

---

45. So Neuman, "Cultic Origins," 48. Contra McIntyre who unfairly cites an exposition of Rom 10:9–10 by Phoebe Palmer from 1848: "But do not forget that believing with the heart, and confessing with the mouth, stand closely connected.... To the degree that you rely on the faithfulness of God, O hasten to make confession with the mouth of your confidence." McIntyre, *E. W. Kenyon and His Message of Faith*, 48. Citing Palmer, *Faith and Its Effects*, 113.

46. McConnell, *A Different Gospel*, 3–13. Geir Lie mentions that Hagin would read Kenyon's books on his radio program and then claim that it was a passage from one of his own books: Lie, "E. W. Kenyon," 60–61.

47. E.g., Hagin, *Real Faith*, 11–12; Hagin, *New Thresholds of Faith*, 8, 89–90; Hagin, *Right and Wrong Thinking*, 25–30; Hagin, *How to Turn Your Faith Loose*, 8–10; Hagin, *What Faith Is*, 5–8; Hagin, *Prayer Secrets*, 1–2, 6–7

48. Hagin, *How to Turn Your Faith Loose*, 14–16; Hagin, *Zoe: The God-Kind of Life*,

God *believed* that what He *said* would come to pass. He spoke the Word, and there was an earth. . . . He said it and it was so! That is the God-kind of faith. . . . Jesus demonstrated the God-kind of faith to His disciples, and then he told them that they, too, had that kind of faith.[49]

He also develops the idea, not only of the imperative of positive confessions, but also of the perils of a negative, or "double" confession:

> Remember, your confession of Satan's ability to keep you from success gives him dominion over you. . . . You see, when you confess your doubts, fears, weakness, and disease, you are openly confessing that God's Word is not true.[50]

He thus tempers Kenyon's optimism about the power of faith by spelling out a little more clearly the limits imposed on Faith by fear and unbelief. He has a high anthropology in which the believer, as the custodian of delegated divine authority is totally responsible for spiritual victory or defeat. In one place Jesus apparently admits to Hagin that He cannot intervene.[51]

The main achievement of Hagin has been to popularize Kenyon's ideas. Through his emphasis on Mark 11:23, he has given Scriptural sanction to what may be described as the logocratic aspect of Kenyon, that is, his belief in the power of spoken words to create reality. The concept of a "positive confession" is fully born.[52] Through this principle of word-power, the stage was set by Hagin for a progressively more formulaic and anthropocentric doctrine of faith. It is in Hagin that this doctrine of faith begins to take on the appearance of a kind of Self-Help Christianity very similar to the ideas of Norman Vincent Peale or Robert Schuller. Hagin has thus bequeathed a pragmatic Christianity to a pragmatic age.

Hagin went on to father every major preacher within the Faith movement. Kenneth Copeland, Charles Capps, Frederick Price and many others,

---

17–20.

49. Hagin, *New Thresholds of Faith*, 81; Hagin, *Your Faith in God Will Work*, 3; Hagin, *Bible Faith Study Course*, 88.

50. Hagin, *How to Turn Your Faith Loose*, 28; Hagin, *Right and Wrong Thinking*, 22–30; Hagin, *New Thresholds of Faith*; *Bible Faith*, 91, 93.

51. "Then I told him [a demon] to get out of there. So he ran off. Jesus said then, 'If you hadn't done that, I couldn't have.'" Hagin, *Authority of the Believer*, 18–19.

52. Hagin, *In Him*, 1: "A spiritual law too few of us realize is: Our confessions rule us." Hagin, Bible Faith, 91: "Realization follows confession. Confession precedes possession"; Hagin, *How to Turn Your Faith Loose*, 23: "Faith's confessions create reality." Also: Hagin, *Words*; Hagin, *You Can Have What You Say*.

acknowledge the formative role Hagin has had in their ministries. The most prominent of these is the man who was soon recognized as the undisputed leader of the Faith movement—Kenneth Copeland.

Kenneth Copeland

In the writings of Hagin, not everything is subsumed within a Faith framework. He has taught on a number of subjects not directly related to the concerns of Faith and with seemingly no desire to make these subjects fit into his schema.[53] Copeland is different. He has a powerful intellect capable of systematizing a complete Faith theology. His retelling of salvation history from Creation, through to the Fall, the Abrahamic Covenant, and the advent and work of Christ is mercilessly mocked in Hanegraaff's *Christianity in Crisis*.[54] Copeland's style is also different. Hagin is winsome and entertaining; Copeland is impetuous and forceful. Copeland is a legalist. His concept of faith is one bound by unalterable cosmic laws that, if obeyed, guarantee an eventual outcome:

> We must understand that there are laws governing every single thing in existence.... It is the force of gravity which makes the law of gravity work. In the same way, spiritual law would be useless if the force of faith were not a real force.... There are certain laws governing prosperity revealed in God's Word. Faith causes them to function.[55]

In Copeland we see some significant aspects of Hagin's teachings brought to new extremes. He adds to Hagin's emphasis on the power of speaking faith-filled words the thought that faith is the force behind those words.[56] Faith is seen as something divine and powerful that is dropped

---

53. E.g. Hagin, *Three Big Words*, this refers to "atonement," "remission" and "forgiveness"; Hagin, *Why Do People Fall Under The Power?*; Hagin, *Learning to Flow With the Spirit of God*; Hagin, *Observations on Fasting*.

54. Hanegraaf, *Christianity in Crisis*, 19–27.

55. E.g. Copeland, *The Laws of Prosperity*, 18–19: Cf. Copeland, *Giving and Receiving*, 22–23: "First, God promised it, so in order to establish His covenant, He has to give you the power to obtain wealth. Secondly, He gives you the seed in order for you to put the covenant into motion. *Giving establishes or sets in motion God's covenant*" (italics original).

56. Copeland, *Force of Faith*, 18: "The force of faith is released by words."

into the recreated "spirit man" of every believer at his or her new birth. God is a Faith God and believers can exercise the God-kind of faith:

> Each time God spoke, He released His faith-creative power to bring His words to pass.... Man was created from the faith-filled words of God—words of power, dominion and life ... all of the power that it took to have dominion over the earth was a part of man from the very beginning.[57]

The flipside of this is that fear is also a force released in words that can bring about negative results.[58] Copeland shares with Kenyon a high anthropology,[59] and a conflation of regeneration with justification.[60]

A contradiction that is more noticeable in his teaching than in Hagin's is that, on the one hand, every word spoken, whether good or bad, whether driven by faith or fear, will bring an inevitable result.[61] On the other hand, for a good result, it is necessary to employ the "power twins" of faith and patience.[62] He thus sometimes speaks of a completely deterministic law of faith or fear and sometimes speaks of the need for personal exertion and commitment to bring a result. When determinism operates and when exertion is required appears to be purely arbitrary. The cosmology implied seems to balance precariously on the border between a mechanistic and hence deterministic and impersonal view of the universe, and a relational and hence indeterminate and animistic view of it. It is Isaac Newton meets tribal witch doctor.

In defense of him, Perriman has described much Word of Faith teaching as "folk religion."[63] Copeland seems to be appealing to a relatively uneducated audience and uses vivid imagery and almost silly terminology to describe how the spiritual laws of faith govern the cosmos.[64] Nevertheless,

---

57. Copeland, *Power of the Tongue*, 5–7.

58. Copeland, *Force of Faith*, 14: "Fear activates Satan the way faith activates God."

59. "Your spirit is just as big as God's because you are born of Him." Copeland, *Walking in the Realm of the Miraculous*, 19.

60. Copeland, *Walking in the Realm of the Miraculous*, 83–84: "The experience of the new birth is the most miraculous event that will ever occur in your life. You were reborn from a death of trespass and sin and made alive unto God. You were recreated and made to be righteousness—a spotless child of the God of heaven and earth."

61. Copeland, *Force of Faith*, 18: "Words bring things to pass. Your words work for you, or they work against you."

62. Ibid., 23–32.

63. Perriman, *Faith, Health and Prosperity*, 16, 100–3, 143, 155.

64. The whole plan of redemption is subsumed within a fantastically commercial

where his concept of faith is concerned, he has so majored on the concept of faith as a creative force that Kenyon's and Hagin's slightly less extreme ideas of faith appear to recede somewhat into the background. This amounts to a lot more than mere Southern preacher's rhetoric.

Charles Capps

Charles Capps took his cue from Hagin's book, *Right and Wrong Thinking*, which deals with the significance of the idea that "you can have what you say." Although Capps's rise to fame was more or less contemporaneous with that of Copeland, his thinking was a clear development on his. Like Copeland, he radicalized many of Hagin's ideas but went a step further still. Charles Capps represents something of a logical terminus in Faith theology. It does not seem possible to take Kenyon's, or Hagin's, or Copeland's ideas to any greater extreme than Capps did.

Capps specialized in the study of words. He made a thorough search of all that the Scriptures teach about the tongue and summarized his findings in a hugely popular book called, *The Tongue: A Creative Force*.[65]

In this book, Capps allows no exceptions to Hagin's "You can have what you say" remit:

> *He said* "THOSE THINGS WHICH HE SAITH"; everything you say, you must watch what you say. You have to believe that those things that you say—everything you say—will come to pass.[66]

Everything in the universe, whether spiritual or physical, is governed by unalterable laws of cause and effect:

> In dealing with the natural law that governs electricity, we have learned that if we work with the law by obeying and enforcing it, that electrical force will work for us. But if we continually violate that law that governs or controls electricity we will get into a *"heap of trouble"* . . . *so are the words that come forth from out of your mouth.*[67]

For Capps, nothing ever happens without words. God spoke the universe into being and since that time has never done anything without

---

rubric in Copeland, *Giving and Receiving*.

65. Capps, *The Tongue*: at least 500,000 copies sold according to the front cover.

66. Ibid., 24 (italics and capitalization his, so throughout).

67. Ibid., 8–9.

saying it first.[68] This is described as God's faith.[69] Man, created in the image of God, has the same creative verbalizing ability.[70] Further, God seemingly cannot intervene into human lives without the spoken word of the person concerned.[71] The devil, likewise, cannot do anything except by means of the negative words of Christians. Their negative speech "establishes" the devil's word in the earth, just as their positive speech can establish God's word in the earth.[72] Like Kenyon and Copeland, Capps also conflates justification with regeneration, leading to a similarly exalted anthropology.[73] With Hagin and Copeland, he also affirms the power of fear as the flipside of faith.[74]

Joyce Meyer

With the first generation of Word of Faith leaders now either dead or growing very old, Meyer, though not exactly youthful herself, deserves in many ways to be viewed as the present day bearer of the Word of Faith mantle. She has softened some of its hard edges and introduced new hard edges of her own. Platform speaking of the kind supplied by Word of Faith teachers seems to cater to an audience that is accustomed to tough, adversarial language. Joyce Meyer, in order to answer to this expectation, needs an enemy, yet the old enemy—unbelief—she has tended to avoid fighting. Her audience is, it seems, discerning enough to expect "balance" in such matters. She assures her readers that, when she faces reasons to be anxious, she believes in "facing facts, having a ready mind and still being positive. *This is balance.*"[75] The new enemy is Satan himself, whom she rails against to such

68. Ibid., 32.

69. Ibid.

70. "There was creative power that flowed out of the mouth of God and you were created in the image of God. Then according to the Scriptures and what Jesus said, you have the same ability dwelling or residing inside of you." Capps, *The Tongue*, 17.

71. "You have said, 'Lord it's getting worse—it's not getting any better.' You have stopped God's ability immediately. Maybe it was just about to come to manifestation but you have established Satan's word in the earth." Capps, *The Tongue*, 79–80.

72. This teaching is derived from 2 Cor.13:1 "By the word of two or three witnesses every word shall be established," i.e., God's word plus the believer's word equals "established." Satan's word plus the believer's equals the same. See Capps, *The Tongue*, 45, 56.

73. "You were once a sinner, but now YOU'RE BORN AGAIN, THE RIGHTEOUSNESS OF GOD." Capps, *The Tongue*, 15.

74. "Fear is the reverse gear of faith . . . faith in the enemy's ability." Capps, *The Tongue*, 56–57.

75. Meyer, *Battlefield of the Mind*, 51. Emphasis original.

an extent that there is a reference to him on most of the pages of *Battlefield of the Mind*.[76] Almost everything that is deemed a hindrance is ascribed to his agency. He has a "plan for our lives,"[77] he uses human emotions,[78] speaks lies into the human mind,[79] and brings believers under feelings of "guilt and condemnation."[80] He destroys faith with his lies,[81] and so on.

Her answer to all of this satanic activity is not monochrome and she often takes on the role of a therapist using quasi-psychological language.[82] However, it is clear that the strategy she would stake her success on is speaking out the Word of God. There is an emphasis on being positive. She uses the simple positive confession, "God loves me," every morning, intensifying its use during periods of doubt, but for the most part, it is the direct citation of memorized verses of Scripture that is held up as the only worthwhile content of such confessions:

> I highly recommend speaking the Word of God out of the mouth ... The Word of God coming forth out of a believer's mouth, with faith to back it up, is the single most effective weapon that can be used to win the war against worry and anxiety.[83]

Her convictions about speaking God's word seem closer to a kind of *lectio divina* than the mechanistic or magical approaches of Copeland or Capps:

> When we confess God's Word out loud, we write it on our own heart, and it becomes more firmly established both in our heart and in the earth. God's Word is forever settled in heaven (see Psalm 119:89), and we establish it in the earth each time we speak it.[84]

---

76. Ibid.
77. Meyer, *Managing Your Emotions*, 13.
78. Ibid., 14.
79. Ibid., 22.
80. Ibid., 33.
81. Meyer, *Battlefield of the Mind*, 107.
82. Meyer, *Managing Your Emotions*.
83. Meyer, *Battlefield of the Mind*, 125.
84. Meyer, *Secret Power of Speaking God's Word*, xviii.

Praying Effectively

However, even when there is no directly Scriptural content, she is clear that "Words are containers for power,"[85] and she can be quite outspoken about this. Note also the new enemy:

> Words are containers that carry either creative or destructive power. Your mouth is a weapon—either for Satan or against him. We can help the devil bring destruction into our lives, or we can learn how to agree with God and experience His best for us.[86]

And here again:

> The mouth gives expression either to the flesh or to the spirit. It can be used to verbalize God's Word or it can be a vehicle to express the enemy's work. I don't believe that any child of God wants to be used as a mouthpiece for the devil, but many are.[87]

She carefully moderates this kind of language however, by stating for instance, that, "obedience and forgiveness are as important as faith and persistence."[88]

Her books certainly seem to suggest a variegated and softened faith message for a less absolutist postmodern audience. She adds to this a profound openness about her own fights of faith, making especially frequent references to her beloved husband, Dave. Despite the scandals that have surrounded the opulent lifestyles of televangelists, she has continued the tradition of owning multiple homes and a private jet but has been careful to comply with requests for financial transparency.

Conclusion

With regards to the origins of the Word of Faith teachers' concept of Faith, I have traced a hundred year long line of thinking from Kenyon, in the late nineteenth and early twentieth centuries, to Meyer in the present day. To trace the line further back than Kenyon with absolute certainty is problematic due to the lack of any references to other works in Kenyon's writings. Yet what is clear is that there are strong similarities between Kenyon's ideas about faith and the teachings of New Thought. What is for sure is that

---

85. Meyer, *The Word, The Name, The Blood*, 37.
86. Meyer, "Your Mouth is a Weapon," 2.
87. Meyer, *Me and My Big Mouth*, 6.
88. Ibid., 10.

something that does not appear to be of Christian origin crept into Kenyon's theology at some point. Kenyon then built a concept of faith around this foreign idea. This element is a belief that a person can possess a creative power above and beyond the natural creative abilities with which men and women are naturally endowed by God. Every believer's goal, therefore, should be to develop and actualize this power.

This belief in born-again human potential is introduced to a wider public by Hagin, who, by emphasizing Mark 11:23, develops and popularizes Kenyon's belief in the need for confession to release the creative power of indwelling Faith. Hagin also develops further the idea, already latent in Kenyon, that negative words have an equal and opposite power to Faith-filled words. Copeland then develops this belief in words as the means of releasing the God-Kind of Faith, seeing Faith as the operator of cosmic law. Copeland affirms, along with Hagin, that Faith can be obstructed by negative confessions. Capps then goes further still, deducing that words are the cause of everything in the universe. By harnessing the power of words, therefore, anything is possible in this universe, whether good or bad, since words create reality. The importance of the speaker of those words is reduced. Finally, in the Joyce Meyer world, we are finally relieved of the hegemony of words and the devil is brought into play. Finally, we can point the finger somewhere other than our tongues, though she does not let us off the hook completely.

Some of the biggest difficulties, as we have seen, arise when reasons have to be found as to why the creative force of Faith does not always succeed in creating anything. The lack of results is traced primarily to unbelief, but both unbelief and Faith must go, cap-in-hand, to the world of words in order to find expression and materialize. If therefore, nothing whatsoever can materialize without words, then it is words that are in control, not the Faith-filled believer, nor the fear-filled doubter.

Further, for a Faith-filled believer to make a difference in a universe in which words become events, he must continually form and contribute as many Faith-filled words as possible into the word-galaxy of life. These words will then have to compete with the vast array of words that, at some point, have been spouted by all those careless people who are not abreast of the laws of Faith. Such people, of course, are in an overwhelming majority. The Faith-filled believer, then, must send his or her words out into the no-man's-land of a hostile universe and hope that somehow, they will bear fruit.

The developments seen in Capps are slightly ironic. Kenyon was an idealist. Indeed, DeArteaga lauds his ideas as an example of "Faith-Idealism."[89] In the light of the findings of quantum physics, argues DeArteaga, some form of Faith-Idealism is the only position a Christian should take.[90] With Capps, however, we have arrived at an opposing philosophical position. No longer is the inner human consciousness (or any aspect of it) the center of the universe as the idealists insisted. Now, in Capps, matters are somewhat out of our hands. The universe is created and sustained, and human lives are prospered or destroyed, entirely by words. It no longer matters so much whose words they are since other people have the power to limit one's potential by their negative confessions.[91] Capps states that words can be "idle" and that only as the relevant laws are obeyed can the power of words be tapped into.[92] Yet because negative speech has to be cited as the reason why Faith does not always accomplish anything, one is left with the same arbitrary determinism versus exertion conflict that Copeland displays. Capps's cosmology, therefore, raises the same question as Copeland's, that concerning when exactly words do "come to pass" and when they do not.

Like most aspects of Charismatic faith, Word of Faith amounts to a critique of late modern materialism, a critique—like Postmodernity itself—of the Enlightenment project but retaining some of the key Enlightenment paradigms such as cause and effect and a quasi-Newtonian belief in universal laws. As part of this critique, Word of Faith insists upon the existence of the supernatural, and also claims the power to be able to control it. Furnishing evidence that this realm has been successfully manipulated is the best way, in fact, of proving its existence. Such evidence would be the palatial homes that the leaders of the movement freely display within the glossy pages of their magazines.[93] Their claim is that were they to give away their wealth, God would give it back to them, perhaps several-fold. They are, in any case, all great believers in the spiritual laws of giving. They gave—often very sacrificially—and God responded by showering them with wealth.

89. DeArteaga, *Quenching the Spirit*, 131–32, 212.

90. Ibid., 161–62: ". . . quantum physics has conclusively shown that the mind inherently has some tiny power, enough to cause light to act like a particle. The real question is how much more power the mind has naturally."

91. Capps, *The Tongue*, 85.

92. Ibid., 9.

93. E.g., almost any issue of Kenneth Copeland Ministries' *Believers' Voice of Victory* magazine. I was given a year's free subscription just for making an enquiry after some sources via the website.

It is important to note here that the Word of Faith system was never intended as a way of selling religion. This is not the aim that lies at the heart of the movement. The various organizations that promote the movement do use commercial models of advertising but no more so than, say, Christian music publishers do. The heart of the movement is deeply spiritual. The material is supposed to give evidence of the immaterial. The health and prosperity of the faithful are intended to point to the realities of the spiritual realm and the potential that exists for a believer to become so attuned to that realm as to be able to exercise power over it.

The Word of Faith tribe is a group with immense claims. The whole universe can only be controlled by people of faith who understand the laws of faith. It is difficult to exaggerate the force of this claim. These are people that see themselves more as exiled kings than resident aliens. Word of Faith is a metaphysic and, despite the apparently brash materialism it espouses, remains resolutely spiritual. It seeks tangible results purely for the sake of its own legitimation. It is a fight of and for "faith" in the midst of an increasingly hostile secular world. Word of Faith is a muscular group that is allergic to any forms of Christianity that cower or huddle in small groups. They are bold and strident and are not excited by simplicity or humility.

Paradoxically, however, the very teachings that promise wonders in response to words are in danger of producing a loss of wonder—a loss of wonder, that is, at the unprompted kindness and benevolence of a God. The Faith idea of faith is, after all, a mere human ability to think and speak positively that is then expected to achieve the super-human. It cannot be proven whether this Creative Faith ever actually produces the results promised. It is equally improbable that such Faith could have been the same power by which God created the universe. What is certain is that it is very hard work to sustain.

For adherents, letting go of this Faith concept may be hard, just as it was, in fact, for Kenneth Copeland to change from his over-rich diet of cakes and sweet things to a love of tossed salad.[94] It is an exchange of false certainty for honest uncertainty—a far less exciting idea once you have gotten used to the glucose highs of thinking you can manipulate the laws of the universe. It was hard for me when I finally let go of it in 2004. Ex-adherents need the good food of a healthy God-concept in place of the over-rich diet of an unhealthy (and exhausting) Faith concept.

---

94. His remarkable story of overcoming gluttony and obesity is candidly told in Copeland, *The Decision*, 17–26.

5

Conquering Evil Forces

SPIRITUAL WARFARE

A Brief History

The cultural context in which Spiritual Warfare theology emerged included such things as the 1959 repeal of the Witchcraft Act, horror films such as *The Exorcist*, rock groups such as the delightful Black Sabbath and equally charming Electric Lucifer, the popularity of Eastern religions, belief in the Age of Aquarius, and the subsequent burgeoning of the New Age movement. All these generated interest in paranormal phenomena.[1] A. Scott Moreau includes *Dungeons and Dragons*, *Ghost Busters*, and *The Haunting* in his list of cultural indicators of a shift towards fascination with spirit beings.[2] The fact that *Harry Potter* is now in its second generation of ardent eight-year-old fans is evidence enough, perhaps, that this interest has not faded.

It is, however, difficult to trace a definite beginning point for Spiritual Warfare. It clearly has antecedents such as in the ministry of Jessie Penn-Lewis. She developed a strong demonological emphasis as early as 1897.[3] She could get quite lyrical about the "unseen forces of the powers of

---

1. Scotland, *Charismatics and the Next Millennium*, 115–16.

2. Scott Moreau, "Gaining Perspective on Territorial Spirits," http://www.lausanne.org/content/territorial-spirits#N_50_.

3. With her *Conflict in the Heavenlies* series: Garrard, *Mrs Penn-Lewis*, 228–29.

darkness,"[4] and the need to "*bind* the devil"[5] Her *War Against the Saints* of 1912, an anti-Pentecostal tirade about the dangers of demonic counterfeits and so forth, represented her demonology at its most developed. Though she coincidentally uses similar terminology to that of the Charismatic movement, I have not found any evidence that Penn-Lewis was very influential upon the early progenitors of Spiritual Warfare methodology.

Wright traces the origins of today's Spiritual Warfare theology to some of the post-World War II healing evangelists such as William Branham, who openly identified and rebuked spirits on stage. Branham influenced Ern Baxter, who, in turn influenced Derek Prince. The publication of Michael Harper's 1970 book, *Spiritual Warfare*, appears to be the moment the term "spiritual warfare" was coined,[6] and as early as 1973, we can see much of the key terminology of spiritual warfare already in use: "spiritual warfare" itself, and "binding and loosing," being used freely, though not without a short explanation, in the Hammonds's *Pigs in the Parlor*.[7] Derek Prince began preaching about the danger of amulets and charms throughout the 1970s and also spoke of "strong men" that rule churches, cities and nations.[8] In 1985, Terry Law, within the Word of Faith movement encouraged his readers to use their mouths as a weapon in warfare praise.[9]

It seems to have been the Frank Peretti novels of the late 1980s that were decisive in shifting the conversation a stage further. His international bestsellers *This Present Darkness* of 1986, and *Piercing the Darkness* of 1989, though works of fiction, comprehensively opened up for readers an unseen world behind the physical world in which demonic spirits do all they can to prevent revival and hamper the work of the Church. And the answer presented was very clear: prayer. Prayer was becoming seen as a way of going on the offensive, a weapon of spiritual battle.

Meanwhile, At Fuller Seminary, Paul Hiebert's landmark article for *Missiology*, "The Flaw of the Neglected Middle,"[10] was already providing a

4. Penn-Lewis, *Life in the Spirit*, 23.
5. Ibid., 19 (italics original).
6. Warren, "'Spiritual Warfare,'" 279.
7. Hammond and Hammond, *Pigs in the Parlor*, 62–63.
8. Wright, "Devil You Think You Know," 90.
9. Law, *Principles of Praise*, pages 145–56 are abridged in Kay and Dyer, *Pentecostal and Charismatic Studies*, 273–74.
10. Hiebert, "Flaw of the Excluded Middle," 35–47. For the full story of this article's seminal but controversial influence, see: Anane-Asane et al., "Paul H. Hiebert's 'The Flaw of the Excluded Middle,'" 189–97

theoretical justification for John Wimber, Peter Wagner, and Charles Kraft to begin formulating a specifically Christian response to the demonic realm: the "power encounter."

The first of the great manuals of Spiritual Warfare, of the kind that would soon become commonplace, appeared in 1989 with John Dawson's influential *Taking Our Cities for God*. Following this, throughout the 1990s, we see C. Peter Wagner seize his moment as the leader of the Spiritual Warfare movement, dominating the field with his elaborate teachings about territorial spirits. By corroborating his insights with stories of numerous evangelistic breakthroughs that seemed to follow strategic and focused prayer campaigns, he was able to articulate the beginnings of a "technology"[11] of prayer-backed evangelism.

The arrival of this technology onto the global scene signaled a clean break from earlier Charismatic demonologies that had been chiefly concerned with the exorcism of individuals. Now, exorcisms were relegated to "ground level" spiritual warfare. Fighting against occultic activity was categorized as "occult-level spiritual warfare," while the third and highest level was dubbed, "strategic-level spiritual warfare" (SLSW).[12] This kind of warfare, sometimes also referred to as "cosmic-level,"[13] was the level that concerned itself with territorial spirits. Territorial spirits were, "high ranking members of the hierarchy of evil spirits" who are given by Satan the responsibility "to control nations, cities, tribes, people groups, neighborhoods and other significant social networks of human beings throughout the world."[14] In the West, as we will see, this teaching challenged the scientific worldview with something very like animism,[15] in its attempt to "re-enchant Protestant Christian cosmology."[16]

More recently, the ongoing importance of Spiritual Warfare to Charismatic understandings of mission has been made clear by the *Transformations* videos and later documentaries directed by George Otis Jr.[17] In

11. Wagner's term.

12. All three levels are introduced for the first time in Wagner, *Warfare Prayer*, 14–17.

13. Kraft, "Spiritual Warfare," 1091–96. Kraft admits of only two levels: "ground" and "cosmic."

14. Wagner, "Territorial Spirits," in Wagner and Pennoyer, *Wrestling with Dark Angels*, 77.

15. Lowe, *Territorial Spirits and World Evangelization*.

16. DeBernardi, "Spiritual Warfare and Territorial Spirits," 66.

17. *Transformations: When God Comes to Town* first appeared in 1999 and was followed in 2001 by *Transformations II: The Glory Spreads*. Both are revivalistic

a similar vein are documentaries from Darren Wilson of Bethel Church, such as *The Finger of God* (2006), *Furious Love* (2009), *Father of Lights* (2012), and *Holy Ghost* (2014). The Darren Wilson documentaries, however, seem to be much more Signs and Wonders orientated and are less about any defined Spiritual Warfare methodology. In addition a number of Peter Wagner's books from the 1990s were re-released by Destiny Image publishing house in 2012.

The story, then, seems to be one of an escalating awareness of evil that moves beyond the exorcism of individuals to the exorcism of homes, meetings, churches, towns, neighborhoods, and nations. Popular Christian publications feeding the theology of spiritual warfare started out as manuals on exorcism before branching out in the 1990s into, literally, taking on the world.[18]

---

documentaries about communities around the world that have been transformed by God. In every case, the cause is found to be the strategic spiritual binding of the territorial spirits dominating the area.

18. Judson Cornwall, *Let us Praise* (1973); Frank and Ida-Mae Hammond, *Pigs in the Parlour* (1973); Graham and Shirley Powell, *Christian Set Yourself Free* (1983); Bill Subritzky, *Demons Defeated* (1985); Frank Peretti, *This Present Darkness* (1986, sold half a million); Graham Kendrick, *Make Way Songbook* (1986); Charles Kraft, *Christianity with Power* (1989); John Dawson, *Taking our Cities for God* (1989); Derek Prince: *Blessing or Curse: You can Choose!* (1990); C. Peter Wagner, *Engaging the Enemy* (1991); Peter Horrobin, *Healing Through Deliverance* (1991); Cindy Jacobs, *Possessing the Gates of the Enemy: A Training Manual for Militant Intercession* (1991); C. Peter Wagner, *Warfare Prayer* (1992); C. Peter Wagner, *Prayer Shield* (1992); Ed Murphy, *A Handbook for Spiritual Warfare* (1992); C. Peter Wagner, *Breaking Strongholds in Your City* (1993); C. Peter Wagner, *Confronting the Powers* (1996); C. Peter Wagner, *Praying With Power* (1997); George Otis Jr. *The Twilight Labyrinth* (1997).

Scholarly work on the subject of Spiritual Warfare has all but ground to a halt, having reached its peak in the 1990s. Since then, it has focused its attention more on exorcistic practice: Wesley Carr, *Angels and Principalities* (1981); Walter Wink, *Naming the Powers* (1984); Andrew Walker, *Enemy Territory* (1987); Nigel Wright, *The Fair Face of Evil* (1989); Paul Hiebert, "Spiritual Warfare: Biblical Perspectives" (1992); Paul Hiebert, *Anthropological Reflections on Missiological Issues* (1994); Andrew Walker, "The Devil You Think You Know: Demonology and the Charismatic Movement" (1995); S. H. T. Page, *Powers of Evil* (1995); Greg Boyd, *God at War* (1997); Clinton Arnold, *3 Crucial Questions about Spiritual Warfare* (1997); Chuck Lowe, *Territorial Spirits and World Evangelization* (1998); D. A. Carson, "God, the Bible and Spiritual Warfare: A Review Article" (1999); Bill Ellis, *Raising the Devil: Satanism, New Religious Movements, and the Media* (2000); James Collins, *Exorcism and Deliverance Ministry in the Twentieth Century: An Analysis of the Practice of Exorcism in Modern Western Christianity* (2009); Graham Russell Smith, "The Church Militant: A Study of 'Spiritual Warfare' in the Anglican Charismatic Renewal" (2011); William Kay and Robin Parry, *Exorcism and Deliverance: Multi-Disciplinary Studies* (2011); E. Janet Warren, "'Spiritual Warfare': A Dead Metaphor?" (2012).

The reasons for this escalation are difficult to pinpoint. It would be easy—probably too easy—to read into this a growing unease, as we entered the 1990s, about the place of Christianity within public life: a growing powerlessness which Spiritual Warfare attempts to compensate for. Yet it is important not to overlook the fact that, within this journey towards full-blown SLSW, there was a recovery of an enriched and perhaps more biblical worldview. It could be that some of these explorations actually bring us closer to the way the earliest Christians viewed the cosmos.

The Spiritual Warfare Worldview

An important beginning point for the development of the theory of Spiritual Warfare is one that is also shared by Signs and Wonders theology. This starting point owes its origins to C. Peter Wagner's and John Wimber's collaboration in the now world-famous but short-lived module: "MC510 Signs and Wonders and Church Growth," at Fuller Theological Seminary. This module ran from 1982–85 and articulated a firm conviction that there are fundamental problems with the scientific worldview of Western people, including Western Christians. This worldview, according to their critique, creates a sharp dichotomy between the natural and the supernatural, which nearly always results in the natural taking precedence and the supernatural being excluded from discussion. This split results in Western Christianity being trapped in a "powerless intellectualism."[19] But there is yet more to it than this simple re-instatement of the supernatural realm.

It is of note that Wagner has a long history as a missionary in Bolivia (1956–71). The key concept that Wagner seems to take from his experiences in the mission field is that of "territoriality." In other words, it is commonplace in non-Western cultures to find that people conceive of spirits presiding over certain places, cities, and regions.[20] These cultures have continued to believe in the Excluded Middle,[21] the zone that is neither com-

---

19. Granberg, "Christianity with Power," 190.

20. Some examples from Central and South America, Zimbabwe, and Mexico are given in *Warfare Prayer*, 95–98. See also these recent studies: Hio-Kee Ooi, "A Study of Strategic-Level Spiritual Warfare from a Chinese Perspective," 143–61, Asamoah-gyadu, "Pulling Down Strongholds," 306–17, Van der Meer, "Strategic Level Spiritual Warfare," 155–66.

21. Writing in a Chinese-Malay context, Hio-Kee Ooi, while not defending SLSW, points out that the forms of Christianity that have been received in South-East Asia have left a void for its adherents in that Chinese Christians are historically part of a culture

pletely earthly nor completely heavenly but which is the world of spirits, of gods and goddesses that share the everyday places of earth with us: the mountains, rivers, and forests. They are earthly yet entirely non-physical beings. This Excluded Middle is the world that, in the West, has tended not to have been taken seriously since the days when stories were told that involved elves, trolls, and fairies.[22] It is also, seemingly, the worldview that sometimes surfaces in the Bible, something that Wagner and others have not been slow to spot, and biblical examples of spiritual territoriality, such as Daniel 10, have been much cited.

Wagner, following Hiebert, made the point that, even when Westerners do include the spiritual or supernatural dimension in their thinking, they do so in an entirely binary way: God and spiritual things are up there, humans, matter, and all earthly things are down here. The arrangement is incomplete, it seems, without this middle zone that is neither completely up there nor totally down here. So we have not only a newly reclaimed supernatural realm but a third realm that is mid-way between the two—and its discovery in practice tends to somewhat eclipse the natural. Natural explanations start to recede quite alarmingly.

Of note has been the very clever way in which Wagner has so freely referenced, not only Hiebert, but many other academic authors in his own work,[23] as though to forestall academic criticism. Indeed, Wagner himself was an established member of the faculty at Fuller Seminary for thirty years (1971–2001), where many faculty members appear to have been supportive of him.[24] And there are undoubtedly some academically defensible aspects of the shift in worldview advocated by Wagner.[25]

---

that does believe in the existence of a world of spirits but their Westernized Christian faith does not allow for it: "Strategic Level Spiritual Warfare from a Chinese Perspective," 144, 160–161.

22. Hiebert dated the disappearance of magic and witchcraft in the West (before its recent resurgence) to the seventeenth century. Hiebert, "Flaw of the Excluded Middle," 39.

23. The references come thick and fast in his *Warfare Prayer*, especially chapter 5.

24. Though see Guelich, "Spiritual Warfare," 33–64. Tensions with the President following an episode circulating around the students about a "green-eyed monster" that Wagner and his wife had confronted in the master bedroom of their house are honestly reported in his *Warfare Prayer*, 77–79.

25. He has written for peer review on the subject: "Territorial Spirits and World Missions," 278–88.

Spiritual Warfare Methodologies

Having discussed the theory, we will now unpack some of the key elements within the technology of Spiritual Warfare. We will look at how it works in practice.

Spiritual Mapping

Spiritual Mapping is a term first coined by George Otis Jr. in 1990. It involves a subtle blend of research into the actual history and sociology of a place on the one hand, and spiritual, prayerful discernment on the other. Insights gained in prayer are often claimed to have been confirmed by the research.

> Spiritual mapping is a means whereby we can see what is beneath the surface of the material world; but it is not magic. It is subjective in that it is born out of a right relationship with God and a love for His world. It is objective in that it can be verified (or discredited) by history, sociological observation and God's word.[26]

One practitioner describes having a gifted "master spy" on his team whose calling it was to spy out places and events normally deemed to be spiritually "dangerous" or taboo. The context was Sweden, and this particular spy boldly infiltrated a spiritist group who were "attempting to revive the ancient religion of the Vikings," together with its gods.[27]

Key questions to ask during a mapping exercise include:

> What are the main gods of the nation? . . . What are the altars, the high places and temples connected with worship to fertility gods? . . . Have political leaders, such as a king, president or tribal chief dedicated themselves to a living god? . . . Has there been bloodshed that pollutes the land? . . . How was the foundation of the city

---

26. Otis, "Overview of Spiritual Mapping," 33.
27. Sjöberg, "Spiritual Mapping," 99.

or nation built?[28] How have God's messengers been received?[29] ... How were the old seats of power built?[30]

Territorial Strongholds

The hoped for result of spiritual mapping exercises is that a territorial stronghold is identified that can be the target of a concerted prayer effort. Otis furnishes three main biblical proof texts for the existence of territorial strongholds—a term that seems to mean much the same as a "territorial spirit"[31]: Deut 32:8; Ezek 28:12–19; Daniel 10; and Eph 6:12.

Testimonies abound in the literature and material of evangelistic breakthroughs following the identification and defeat of territorial spirits. Just one among many would be the frustrations of a YWAM evangelism team working at the 1978 World Cup in Cordoba, Argentina. The fans were completely indifferent to the efforts of the evangelists. A day of fasting and prayer at a nearby monastery revealed the "principality" called Pride. The residents of Cordoba were, "sophisticated, fashion-conscious and materialistic." They, "cling to values of position, possessions and appearance."[32] From this insight they developed a strategy: to practice humility. This involved kneeling down onto the cobblestones of the streets in the central shopping district, and bowing low with their heads touching the ground. This spectacle drew many onlookers and provided the catalyst for preaching and ministry on the streets.[33] This YWAM team interestingly demonstrates an already quite developed view of "principalities" and how to deal with them long before the Wagner-dominated literature began to dictate terminology and methods. This episode is also notable for the practical action that was taken. More commonly, the strategy centers on prayer rather than symbolic

---

28. For example, Sydney apparently was founded following the massacre of an entire aboriginal tribe: Sjöberg, "Spiritual Mapping," 112.

29. The example is given of a Malaysian town that had not received Francis Xavier, in response to which, Xavier shook off the soles of his feet against it. The pastors of the town, once this was made known, gathered to repent on behalf of the town. A breakthrough in church growth soon followed. Sjöberg, "Spiritual Mapping," 113.

30. Sjöberg, "Spiritual Mapping," 110–14.

31. It would appear to be any "concentration of demonic power." Wagner, *Warfare Prayer*, 16.

32. Lawson, "Defeating Territorial Spirits," 56.

33. Ibid., 55–56.

action: "Social structures, like demonized human beings, can be delivered from demonic oppression through warfare prayer," says Wagner, "History belongs to the intercessors."[34]

Perhaps the aspect of this teaching that is the most disconcerting is the high level of personification of evil powers and the very high level of specificity with which the demonic hierarchies and their strategies are described—descriptions that can seem somewhat imaginative. The following example is not unusual:

> Demons are very conscious of authority and adhere slavishly to the chain of command and the line of authority structure. There are Chief Kings and Chief Princes, and under them are Kings and Princes who rule various geographical and spiritual areas. There are kingdoms, principalities, dominions and powers which are administered by Kings and Princes. Each state in the United states [sic] is ruled over by a prince. Louisiana is ruled by Southern Curses.[35]

These strongholds are then dealt with by such techniques as prayer walking, marching for Jesus, and the novel concept of "Identificational Repentance" in which participants repent on behalf of the sins of a nation or people group, part of "standing in the gap" for them. The response called for almost invariably, however, does not involve trusting in God. Spiritual Warfare shares with other Charismatic theologies the insistence that God has entrusted to believers the power and authority to deal with evil. The main rule of the game tends to be that God refuses to intervene directly. Instead, he equips his people with powerful tools that they must learn to use:

> The devil controls the kingdoms of the world and we are not to underestimate his influence and power, nor believe that this is the will of God. God is telling us to "stand" against these evil forces by equipping ourselves with the power of God, and looking unto Christ as our example.[36]

---

34. Wagner, *Warfare Prayer*, 91.

35. Moody and Moody, *Deliverance Manual*. http://www.demonbuster.com/demonich.html.

36. Magdelene, "Principalities-Powers-Rulers."

Evaluations

I am by no means the first to have done this but a good place to start as we sift through the various evaluations of Spiritual Warfare that have been offered is to draw from the wisdom of C. S. Lewis as expressed in his introduction to *The Screwtape Letters*:

> There are two equal and opposite errors into which our race can fall about the devils. One is to disbelieve in their existence. The other is to believe, and to feel an excessive and unhealthy interest in them. They themselves are equally pleased by both errors, and hail a materialist and a magician with the same delight.[37]

Lewis here gives us some parameters that are extremely helpful as we seek to locate where we might position ourselves in relation to Spiritual Warfare. There seem to have been three main criticisms levelled at Spiritual Warfare, each involving the over-stretching or over-reaching of an idea that is otherwise broadly accepted, namely the personality of evil, the metaphor of Spiritual Warfare and the biblical basis. However, in defense of Lewis' other parameter, I will argue that, while Spiritual Warfare undoubtedly does overplay these three things, it is only because the Western worldview has so underplayed the role of the demonic.

Overstretched Personality

> A born-again army requires a born-again enemy. . . . For too many Christians, especially on the "enthusiastic" wing of the church, the idea of the devil is where they get their energy from.[38]

Nigel Wright is clear that the right way to think of evil is not to give it a personality. He believes it is better to think of the devil as a "non-person, as sub-personal, or anti-personal, rather than personal."[39] Inspired by Barth's concept of "nothingness," he insists that evil is "that about which nothing positive can be said or thought. It exists in negation and is itself wholly negative."[40] Evil as a kind of illegitimate, parasitic non-being has a

---

37. Lewis, *Screwtape Letters*, 9.
38. Wright, "Deliverance and Exorcism," 204.
39. Ibid., 205.
40. Ibid., 208. Those of an apophatic bent would say much the same about God, of course, but with a different end point: A God defined wholly in negation nonetheless turns out to be positive in some way, though not necessarily "good" in any humanly

long history in Christian thought.[41] Similarly, Warren suggests that, rather than thinking of demons as a complex, hierarchical, and well-organized army with a strategy to be outwitted, we should perhaps think of them rather as "chaotic, disorderly, and parasitic on humans."[42] One wonders, however, whether this "non-being" solution is, to all intents and purposes, only a thinly disguised materialism, which Lewis assumes to be the logical consequence of affirming the non-existence of demons. Such an approach also fails to do justice to the ministry of Jesus as portrayed by the writers of the Synoptic Gospels. There seems no reason to contest, for instance, McDermott's assertion, for instance, that "Jesus saw himself as locked in combat with the Evil One, Satan or the Devil."[43] George Eldon Ladd, highly influential on Wimber, defined the Kingdom of God concept not only in terms of the already/not yet tension for which he became well known but also in terms of an unquestionably demonological setting: "The kingdom of God is the redemptive rule of God in Christ defeating Satan and the powers of evil and delivering men from the sway of evil."[44] To describe the demonic in terms only of negation seems to do a disservice to what has been highlighted by broad consensus as a central aspect of Christ's ministry.

However, it could be argued that the result of over-personalizing the devil and naming all of his supposed hierarchies and chains of command is that we end up frozen to the spot—so over-awed by this intelligent and organized enemy that we do nothing but pray. There is concern, in particular, that as this doctrine takes root in African Pentecostal churches, where it finds a ready home, it becomes a substitute for social action. Erwin van der Meer complains that many Southern African Christians are far more likely to hold all night prayer meetings in which territorial spirits are bound than they are to take action against the socio-economic problems that surround them.[45] He suggests some similarities to third- and fourth-century Gnosticism, arguing that too was an escapist other-worldly preoccupation at a time of similar political disturbance and fear.[46] Van der Meer is able to catalogue a number of instances when, for example, a team of African prayer

---

understood sense.

41. See the rest of Wright's chapter for a helpful overview of these.
42. Warren, "'Spiritual Warfare,'" 297.
43. McDermott, *Word Become Flesh*, 45.
44. Ladd, "Kingdom of Christ, God, Heaven," 608.
45. Van der Meer, "Strategic Level Spiritual Warfare," 162.
46. Ibid., 157.

warriors undertook a journey, at great expense, all the way through Africa to the Middle East. The aim was to create a spiritual corridor, binding as they went the territorial spirits that have held Africa for so long.[47] Meanwhile the socio-economic problems of Zimbabwe are attributed to spirits called Nehanda, Chaminuka, Kaguvi, and a crocodile spirit that rules over Harare itself.[48]

In a similar vein to van der Meer's critique, Lausanne found that a preoccupation with spiritual warfare "can lead to avoiding personal responsibility for our actions."[49] This, according to A. Scott Moreau, the author of the Lausanne position paper on territorial spirits, is due to the way SLSW causes participants to no longer see themselves and their sin as part of the problem: "by and large the enemy is externalized, enabling us to avoid responsibility for our sin."[50] And it is undoubtedly the case that the more the unseen evil powers of the world are given names and personalities, the more this kind of projection of blame and responsibility becomes possible. It can even be seized upon as a simplistic theodicy that we think absolves us of the need to explain a loving God active in a world of evil: "It's not God, it's the devil."

An Overstretched Metaphor

It has been pointed out how potentially problematic it is ethically that, if God is a "warrior-God" as in the portrayal of Greg Boyd's *God at War*, for instance, then, God is essentially violent, and humans are therefore made in the image of a violent God.[51] It is pointed out that too little attention has been paid to the fact that, before Spiritual Warfare ever became a "movement," it was only a metaphor, a figure of speech.[52] Like any figure of speech we are supposed to allow it to be limited by an inevitable "is" and "is not"

---

47. Ibid., 161–62.

48. Ibid., 162.

49. Scott Moreau, "Gaining Perspective on Territorial Spirits." http://www.lausanne.org/content/territorial-spirits#N_2_. Going slightly against this assumption, however, is Kay's study which showed that: "the demon worldview engages in or supports social action. . ." Kay, "Demonised Worldview," 27–28.

50. http://www.lausanne.org/content/territorial-spirits#N_50_.

51. Warren, "'Spiritual Warfare,'" 286–87.

52. Guelich, "Spiritual Warfare," 34.

tension.[53] In other words, there is plenty about Spiritual Warfare *as metaphor* that is not remotely similar to actual warfare. The danger, therefore, in extrapolating from the phrase an elaborate technology of practices is that we press the metaphor too far. And warfare is an especially dangerous metaphor to be pressing too far!

One can clearly see this danger in some of the practices, with their overt and imperialistic territoriality. For instance, Ed Silvoso recommends dealing with a city given over to evil by performing a "spiritual takeover," following an infiltration of "Satan's perimeter."[54] After this infiltration, one must launch an "air attack" of intercessory prayer undertaken by thousands of "prayer cells." This has the effect of weakening Satan's control ahead of the "frontal assault," which culminates in evangelism and the discipling of new believers within small groups throughout the city. This approach could be seen as glamorizing, and potentially theologizing, some of the rather less savory aspects of American foreign policy. Those who use this kind of language are, perhaps, not very likely to oppose the idea of American armed forces literally doing this in the name of a combat against evil.

Concerns have been raised when prayer warriors have gone in "all guns blazing" to conduct spiritual warfare around temples and shrines,[55] or to bind the spirits that keep Muslims in the clutches of Satan.[56] Most notorious of these was the trip to the ancient site of Ephesus by a team of prayer warriors to take on the Queen of Heaven. Only in response to widespread complaints did the organizers change the name of the trip from "Operation Queen's Palace" to "Celebration Ephesus."[57] This, thankfully has been followed by the Reconciliation Walk of YWAM's Lynn Green, which would seem to be a far more appropriate way of reaching out to the Middle East.

On the positive side, while it might be easily assumed that anxiety so fills the minds of those who live with this "paranoid universe,"[58] that they would lack any concern for social justice, the truth would appear to

---

53. Warren supplies a brief history of the study of metaphor in religious language: Warren, "'Spiritual Warfare,'" 284–86.

54. Lorenzo "Evangelizing a City Dedicated to Darkness," in Wagner, *Breaking Strongholds in Your City*, 181–82.

55. Lampman, "Targeting Cities with 'Spiritual Mapping' Prayer."

56. Van der Meer, "Strategic Level Spiritual Warfare," 165.

57. DeBernardi, "Spiritual Warfare and Territorial Spirits," 79.

58. Wright, "Devil You Think You Know," 86–105.

be otherwise.[59] Kay's findings were that those who are most prone to this highly aggressive style of spirituality do indeed show high levels of psychoticism. That is, they are likely to be "tough-minded," or to be "lacking empathy"[60] in terms of their personality type. However, it seems this aggressiveness does have its uses: it that can be and is put to work in practical efforts to eliminate social evils.

Further, in defense of Spiritual Warfare as a concept, a case can be made that the manner of God's warfare against evil or Satan is specifically non-violent.[61] It is on an altogether different plain to human warfare and its terrible violence.[62] A problem, however, that the influence of postmodern hermeneutics gives us is the fact that, following Foucault and Derrida, violence can be read into practically everything and need not involve anything physical. Hence violence can be merely ideological, and power can be exercised at a purely linguistic level. This new take on violence potentially gives Spiritual Warfare practitioners who write about "spiritual takeovers" and "frontal assaults" a whole new layer of questions to answer. Walter Wink, instead of "frontal" attacks points us to the finished work of the cross and our participation in it as the ultimate act of non-violent resistance:

> One does not become free from the Powers by defeating them in a frontal attack. Rather, one dies to their control. Here also the cross is the model: we are liberated, not be striking back at what enslaves us—for even striking back reveals that we are still determined by its violent ethos—but by dying out from under its jurisdiction and command.[63]

---

59. Kay, "A Demonised Worldview," 17–29.

60. Ibid., 27.

61. Interestingly, it has been thinkers within the Peace Church tradition that, despite their ardent pacifism, have been at the forefront of reclaiming overtly demonological and militaristic versions of atonement theory—of the patristic "ransom to Satan" variety, in the interests of advancing a specifically non-violent vision of the work of Christ. See my *Atonement Theories*, 1–25, 153–61, for more description of these approaches.

62. The lingering problem then would be how to explain the way God seems to justify extreme violence at a number of places in the Hebrew Scriptures. A number of commendable treatments of this difficulty have appeared in recent years, including: Cowles, *Show Them No Mercy*, Boustan, Jassen and Roetzel, *Violence, Scripture, and Textual Practice in Early Judaism and Christianity*, Copan and Flannagan, *Did God Really Command Genocide?*

63. Wink, *Engaging the Powers*, 157.

Overstretched Biblical Support

It is accepted by some, though not all, that territoriality is a biblical concept. Clinton Arnold supports the theory behind SLSW, but not the practice: "The biblical and historical evidence supports the idea that there are 'territorial spirits.' These are fallen angels that wield some kind of dominion over people groups, empires, countries, or cities," adding, "The evidence does not appear to suggest a strategy for dealing with territorial spirits similar to what some are proposing today."[64] Chuck Lowe, however, denies support for either the theory or the practice of SLSW: "From all angles—biblical, theological, historical, sociological, or empirical—there is little to commend either the theory of territorial spirits or the practice of warfare prayer."[65] There are concerns that this element seems exaggerated in spiritual warfare methods:

> Caution must be exercised lest we exceed the biblical teaching on spiritual warfare. The people of God in both the Old Testament and the New are recorded as responding to the evil spiritual world by recognizing that God alone is God . . .[66]

The danger seems to be that by over-reaching in this way we stray into something very like Gnosticism or animism.[67] In fact some critics have traced this animistic bent directly to Paul Yonggi Cho, who influenced John Dawson prior to the writing of his *Taking Our Cities for God* of 1989. Native Korean spirituality is steeped in shamanism and there are concerns that Cho has syncretized these elements with his Christianity.[68] Indeed the very practice of naming spirits and then binding them is shamanistic.[69] Wagner's defense of the practice of naming territorial spirits is simple: he claims that, if Jesus asked the demons terrorizing the Gadarene man for their names (Mark 5:9), then why should not this same approach be extended from the individual demoniac to the demonized city or nation?[70]

---

64. Arnold, *3 Crucial Questions*, 159
65. Lowe, *Territorial Spirits and World Evangelization*, 130.
66. Greenlee, "Territorial Spirits Reconsidered," 513.
67. Ibid.
68. Biblical Discernment Ministries, "Paul (David) Yonggi Cho: General Teachings/Activities," http://www.rapidnet.com/~jbeard/bdm/exposes/cho/general.htm.
69. DeBernardi, "Spiritual Warfare and Territorial Spirits, 78.
70. Wagner, *Warfare Prayer*, 83–4.

But not only is the biblical basis for the existence of territorial spirits exaggerated, there seems still less biblical (or historical[71]) justification for the practice of spiritual warfare as a precursor to evangelism.[72] This, in turn, points to another concern, namely, the suspicion that this practice is not really based on the Bible primarily. Rather, it is mainly based on a catalogue of anecdotal experiences that are retold at conferences and in books—mainly experiences in the mission field in the context of animistic cultures.[73]

Biblical scholar Clinton Arnold concludes,

> Although God has given us the responsibility of exercising our authority in Christ over unclean spirits that afflict individuals, there is no biblical evidence that God has given us responsibility to bind, expel, or thwart the territorial rulers.[74]

The Lausanne position paper, following a list of very charitable and generous points of praise and agreement, asserts as its very first objection:

> Whatever our conclusion as to whether or not spirits are assigned territories, perhaps the biggest obstacle to SLSW is that the fundamental strategy is not found biblically or in church history, at least not without some serious stretching of the accounts.[75]

Even with regards to the strongest biblical precedent for SLSW, Daniel 10, the use of this passage as a basis for Spiritual Warfare praxis has been easily refuted exegetically: "Daniel did not engage in aggressive prayer against such powers with the expectation of 'binding' or 'evicting' them. The prophet did not pray *against* cosmic powers but *for* the people of God."[76]

The question hangs in the air, however, that Hiebert first so momentously asked, little realizing the fantastical ways in which Spiritual Warfare practitioners would soon answer it: "What is a Christian theology of ancestors, of animals and plants, of local spirits and spirit possession, and of 'principalities, powers and rulers of the darkness of this world' (Eph 6:12)?" It is only later, after Wimber, Kraft, and Wagner had taken Hiebert's question and answered it with a kind of Christian animism that Hiebert clarified

---

71. Lowe, *Territorial Spirits*, chapter 6.
72. DeBernardi, "Spiritual Warfare," 79, referencing Lowe, *Territorial Spirits*, 26–28.
73. DeBernardi, "Spiritual Warfare," 80.
74. Arnold, *3 Crucial Questions*, 197–98.
75. http://www.lausanne.org/content/territorial-spirits#N_50_.
76. Stevens, "Daniel 10," 430.

his own view. It is a view already hinted at in his "Excluded Middle" essay where he makes clear how the Hebrew Bible portrays God as triumphant over such gods of the middle zone as the Ashtoreths and the Baals.[77] He is later even clearer that, in his view, there is a big difference between a biblical worldview and an animistic one. The biblical worldview is of a "divinely ordained and maintained created order" of which the spirit beings of the middle zone are a part. They are mere creatures and are entirely subject to their creator. The animistic worldview, by contrast, is a world in relation to which God is distant and deistic and humans are left to fend for themselves against evil spirits using whatever prayers and charms are deemed effective. It is a world in which "Power, not truth, is the central human concern."[78] Hiebert was clearly concerned that SLSW had gone beyond any biblical retrieval to become unhelpfully animistic.

He offers, however, one olive branch of hope for Charismatics in that he points out how the most successful forms of Christianity within animistic cultures are those that are able to point the most clearly to an intermediary that inhabits the middle zone and can control at an intimate level the everyday hopes and fears of people. In Roman Catholicism this has taken the form of the interceding saints. In Pentecostal and Charismatic expressions of Christianity, the Holy Spirit is readily adopted as fulfilling this role.[79] This also, perhaps, points the way to a New Testament theology of the middle zone. The gift of the Holy Spirit was itself a more than adequate answer for the magic and witchcraft dominated cultures in which Paul planted his most successful churches.

Conclusion

From the above it seems clear that if we overstretch the personality of evil forces we could end up over-awed, excessively fascinated and probably rather intimidated. Retreat from the world into the prayer meeting is clearly a danger. The evidence is not solid, however, and it is clear that Christians steeped in this way of thinking do engage in social action as

---

77. Hiebert, "Flaw of the Excluded Middle," 41.

78. Hiebert, *Anthropological Reflections*, 224. As many as eight other publications by Hiebert that clarify his position are interacted with here: Anane-Asane et al., "Paul Hiebert's 'The Flaw of the Excluded Middle,'" 189–97.

79. Hiebert, "Flaw of the Excluded Middle," 46. An MPhil I supervised on British-Ghanian Pentecostalism bears this out: Nyanni, "Spirit Baptism and Power," 48–53.

well as spiritual war, a two-pronged attack that is at least as old as William and Catherine Booth and the Salvation Army. Yet one wonders whether over-personalizing evil like this is giving some Christians more of a fight on their hands than they need, and whether the energy spent naming, binding and rebuking could be better spent in other ways. Bold faith can quickly become exhausted and anxious faith.

It also seems clear that spiritual warfare is a valid metaphor for the *punctata spiritualis* familiar to serious-minded Christians from time immemorial, yet any metaphor can be pressed too far. While the danger of over-personalizing is intimidation, the danger of overstretching this metaphor is that we find ourselves in an ethical minefield. Muslims could misunderstand, violence could be seen as a divine attribute, actual military invasions might be supported too readily, the cross could be forgotten and the humble ability to accept the things we cannot change could fall before the crusading determination to go on the offensive together against everything we don't like. I am doubtless catastrophizing yet there is clearly a need to be reminded that there is a limit to which any prayer warrior can ever actually be understood to be at war. It is often enough said: "the battle belongs to the Lord."

Lastly, while the danger of over-personalizing is intimidation, and the danger of metaphor-stretching is an ethical minefield, the danger of overstretching the biblical evidence is that it silences the critical faculties of the participants. All participants place a very high value on the authority of Scripture and, once anecdotal evidence is put together with a passage from the Bible, there is a framework of legitimation that participants are likely to find hard to break out of. A particular view, together with its attendant apparatus of naming, binding and loosing, is thus continually reinforced. The danger then, paradoxically, is that what we end up with is discovered to be not at all a biblical worldview but a decidedly animistic one which potentially puts God further away from people's lives, immersing them instead into a scary world of angels and demons which they have to navigate their way through using "discernment."

Having said all of this, the reinstatement of our awareness that there are multiple causes: human, natural and spiritual, to the evils that confront us is important. To realize that there may be demonic as well as human forces at work in the atrocities that we see, provides us all with crucial insights as to how we might pray and act. As with most Pandora's Boxes, however, once it is open things are not safe anymore. The realm of the numinous frightens us. We prefer the world that Pickstock describes where we have eradicated the unknown, choreographed spontaneity and anticipated all eventualities.[80] The realm of the Excluded Middle makes us aware that we are not in control. Once this other world is opened up we know we can no longer rest on Enlightenment reassurances. What we can rely on, however, is the intimate involvement of the creator of this middle zone who has sent his Holy Spirit to guide, protect and empower.

It is hard enough for a culture still fairly dominated by a Hobbesian view of the universe made entirely of "body," to reconcile itself to the existence of a living and personal God and of a divine realm. To then go even further and plea for the recognition of an earthly zone of good and evil spirits, and further still, to assert some proficiency at naming and dealing with these spirits, sounds to Western ears like the path to insanity. This scary new world, the Charismatics have bravely taken on.

---

80. Pickstock, *After Writing*, 3.

Excursus

How do they Grow?

CHARISMATIC EVANGELISM

Charismatics are perhaps better known for their prowess at transfer-growth than they are for any success at evangelism, but evangelize they do. In fact, Pentecostalism as a whole presents us with three different evangelistic methods, each one responsive to the culture of the day. The Classical Pentecostals achieved great success with the evangelistic crusade model that had been pioneered by James Caughy, Charles Finney, D. L. Moody, R. A. Torrey, and then Billy Graham. The Pentecostals had their healing evangelists who emulated these methods but differed from them in the expectation that miraculous signs would confirm the message preached.[1] This style I am calling "Invading" because it sets itself up in the center of urban life and boldly proclaims the gospel there. Today, the baton of the very large, ostentatious healing and miracle crusade is carried by German Pentecostal Reinhard Bonnke and his Christ for All Nations organization.

The Charismatic Renewal perfected a new method that was more suitable to a generation who were less likely to respond to the crusading approach. Initiated by Demos Shakarian[2] and further developed by Alpha,[3]

---

1. For an exhaustive history and prehistory but which sadly does not cover the post-World War II period, see James Robinson's trilogy: *Divine Healing: The Formative Years: 1830–1890*, *Divine Healing: The Pentecostal-Holiness Transition Years: 1890–1906*, *Divine Healing: The Years of Expansion, 1906–1930, Theological Variation in the Transatlantic World*.

2. Read his story in Shakarian, *The Happiest People on Earth*.

3. There is extensive literature analyzing the Alpha phenomenon: Ward, "Alpha—the

the "Inviting" approach used warm, relaxed hospitality to give people a taste of what it would be like to belong within the kind of community for which they longed.

Lastly, the Neo-Charismatics have perfected the use of Signs and Wonders, of being "naturally supernatural" as a way of evangelizing the otherwise indifferent and busy world of shoppers and commuters. People are forced to stop and take note of a wonder: an act of supernatural kindness. This I am describing as "Infiltrating." To this we now turn.

Signs and Wonders as "Tactic"

Cultural studies expert Michel de Certeau, was highly influential in his definition of the way individuals live out their lives in the context of potentially repressive structures imposed by big business, government, even town planners. The big organizations of urban life are the producers. The rest of us are the consumers. The big organizations can strategize from a large and secure power base. Individual consumers may only deploy tactics in a context that they have little control over: "A tactic is a calculated action determined by the absence of a proper locus. . . . The space of a tactic is the space of the other."[4] A tactic has to do with ". . . terrain imposed on it and organized by the law of a foreign power." A tactic involves taking advantage of the ". . . cracks that particular conjunctions open in the surveillance of the proprietary powers. It poaches in them. It creates surprises in them."[5]

Stanley Hauerwas has noted the importance of this image in reflections about the role of the church post-Christendom as its members adopt the attitude of "resident aliens." Inspired by De Certeau, he believes that the church's role is to equip its members for tactics. The days of strategy are passing away: the church has less and less of a secure base of operations from which to strategize. It must be tactical and opportunistic. It must engage selectively with the culture that now surrounds it.[6]

McDonaldization of Religion?"; Hand, *Falling Short?*; Hunt, *Anyone for Alpha?*; Hunt, *The Alpha Enterprise*; Booker and Ireland, *Evangelism: Which Way Now?*; Rooms, "'Nice Process, Shame about the Content'"; Brian, "Researching Alpha"; Brookes, *Alpha Phenomenon*; Heard, *Inside Alpha: Explorations in Evangelism*.

 4. De Certeau, *Practice of Everyday Life*, 36.

 5. Ibid., 36–37.

 6. Hauerwas, *Against the Nations*, 16–17.

Signs and wonders have been shown to "create surprises" in the heart of culture as believers move amongst people in Californian shopping malls armed with words of knowledge or bring prophecies to people on the streets of New York. These are tactical, opportunistic moves; they are infiltrations. They assume no base of operations from which to devise a grand strategy for re-evangelizing the West.

The technical name for one of the most successful Sings and Wonders tactics is Treasure Hunting,[7] developed by Bethel Church, in Redding, California, which is the home of Bill Johnson's enormously popular ministry as well as the increasingly influential Jesus Culture worship band. A Treasure Hunt is a group of faith-filled young people at Bethel that gather together on a Sunday evening to pray. They together wait upon the Lord for words of knowledge. These usually come in the form of a mental picture. Normally little is disclosed of any specific needs that they will encounter. Rather, various relatively trivial details are disclosed such as a mental picture of someone wearing a particular type or color of clothing or other distinguishing visual feature. They then set off for the local mall, armed with a written list, and look out for the people with the features they have seen. Almost invariably, the people they saw in prayer are noticed walking along and are approached with the offer of prayer. The team will be open and honest, showing the person the list on which they appear and explaining how God gave them the list. Often, further details are then revealed, whether supernaturally or otherwise, that help to direct the praying.[8] Sometimes miracles of healing reportedly take place there and then. Almost always, the people they approach are far from hostile and glad to receive prayer. The treasure, according to Dedmon, is the people themselves. They are: ". . . people who had been buried in loneliness, pain, and hopelessness who, when uncovered by the Holy Spirit's leading, were saved, healed, and delivered . . ."[9] The gift of the word of knowledge is the "spiritual metal detector."[10] Dedmon compares the approach to test-driving a car before purchase: a demonstration of the car's capabilities is needed. In the same way, people might need

---

7. There is a handbook on treasure hunting: Dedmon, *The Ultimate Treasure Hunt*.

8. The form of the prayer is mostly based on Matt 6:10, the two key areas being the coming of the Kingdom and the phrase, "on earth as it is in heaven," which forms the basis of Bill Johnson's ministry.

9. Dedmon, *Ultimate Treasure Hunt*, 25.

10. Ibid., 52.

a "demonstration of power."[11] He quotes Bill Johnson: "We owe the world an encounter."[12]

The Healing on the Streets model is a similar tactic, originating in 2005 with Causeway Coast Vineyard Church in Ireland.[13] Improvised versions of the model, involving some other form of signage plus a variety of seating, are common. Locally to me, a Vineyard church offers a set of ultra-relaxing leather sofas to tired shoppers along with their offers of prayer for healing. Meanwhile, another nearby church has been under pressure from the local Secular Society to ensure that they are not promising supernatural healing to anyone but simply offering to pray.

The performance of signs and wonders is often, and quite defensibly, couched in altruistic terms as an act of unconditional mercy towards a needy person. Heidi Baker (together with John and Carol Arnott, Randy Clark, and Bill Johnson) is a member of the Revival Alliance, a loose affiliation of like-minded conference speakers. She is arguably the most outstanding example of a practitioner within this movement who is also mission-minded. She is renowned for her ministry among the poor of Mozambique. Love for the poor seems to be the main motive behind all aspects of her ministry there,[14] and her book *Compelled by Love* is structured around the eight beatitudes of Christ.[15] There is a quest for simplicity and self-emptying which functions alongside an apparently regular success in praying for the deaf, the blind and the crippled in Mozambique.

This new development in Pentecostal-Charismatic evangelism is a very promising one. It is neither the big and brash tent crusade, nor the more craven and retiring hospitality approach. It is bold yet largely inoffensive; totally surprising yet genuinely compassionate. It is born out of what I view as the most promising of the Charismatic critiques of late modernity, the Signs and Wonders movement. To this we now turn.

---

11. Ibid., 54.
12. Ibid., 55.
13. http://www.healingonthestreets.com/mark-marx/.
14. http://www.christianitytoday.com/ct/2012/may/miracles-in-mozambique.html; http://www1.cbn.com/700club/heidi-baker-intimacy-miracles.
15. Baker and Pradhan, *Compelled by Love*.

6

Demonstrating a Living God

SIGNS AND WONDERS[1]

Phase 1: Signs and Wimber

John Wimber was born in 1934 and converted as a jazz musician in 1963. By 1970 he was ordained into the Society of Friends. He never lost his Quaker quietist tendencies, Wimber being more content that most of his contemporaries in ministry to allow for times of silence and minimal human intervention in his meetings. In 1975, he became the Church Growth Consultant for Peter Wagner's Fuller Institute of Evangelism and Church Growth.

---

1. Selected scholarly sources include: Bridge, *Power Evangelism and the Word of God* (1987); Doyle et al., *Signs & Wonders and Evangelicals* (1987); Sarles, "An Appraisal of the Signs and Wonders Movement" (1988); Williams, *Signs, Wonders, and the Kingdom of God* (1989); Bond, *Signs and Wonders: Perspectives on John Wimber's Vineyard* (1990); Shepherd, *A Critical Analysis of Power Evangelism as an Evangelistic Methodology of the Signs and Wonders Movement* (1991); Pratt, "The Need for Dialogue" (1991); Tharp, *Signs and Wonders in the Twentieth Century Evangelical Church* (1992); Algera, *Signs and Wonders of God's Kingdom* (1993); Packer et al., *The Kingdom and the Power* (1993); Menzies, "A Pentecostal Perspective on 'Signs and Wonders.'" (1995).

Selected practitioner sources include: Wimber, *Signs and Wonders and Church Growth* (1984); Wimber and Springer, *Power Evangelism* (1986); Wimber and Springer, *Power Healing* (1986); Wimber and Springer, *Power Encounters* (1988); Wagner, *The Third Wave of the Holy Spirit* (1988); Wimber and Springer, *Power Points* (1991); Deere, *Surprised by the Power of the Spirit* (1993); Johnson, *When Heaven Invades Earth* (2003); Bentley, *The Journey into the Miraculous* (2008); Johnson, *Hosting the Presence* (2012).

He was influenced at this time by reports of healing and deliverance from Latin America, by Wagner's *Look out! The Pentecostals are Coming*, as well as by the writings of Donald Gee and Morton Kelsey. In 1977 he became pastor of Anaheim Vineyard Church, California, a totally independent venture. In 1978, he started praying for the sick with initially no success but he kept going and began to see some remarkable results.

By around 1980 the Charismatic Renewal had died down. Neo-Charismatic networks too had reached a natural summit of expansion and energy and people were looking for something new. The *Mission Course 510 Signs, Wonders and Church Growth* module ran at Fuller Seminary between 1982 and 1985, and was remarkable for the demonstrations in class of God actually performing miraculous healing and deliverance. During this time Wimber's Anaheim Vineyard Church grew to five thousand members. The Vineyard movement which eventually resulted became identified with the term "Third Wave" to describe evangelicals who skewed the identity of "Pentecostal" and who make no claim to have received a baptism in the Holy Spirit in the sense prescribed by Pentecostals yet reserve the right to use the gifts of the Spirit. They would claim, too, to be filled with the Spirit but identify Spirit-reception entirely with conversion, describing supposed baptisms of the Spirit as a welling up from within of an endowment already received at conversion.

Despite Wagner's portrayal of broad support within Fuller, the *Signs, Wonders and Church Growth* course created sufficient controversy at Fuller to warrant a moratorium on its delivery, which was called by David Hubbard, the then president, in 1986.[2] This was in response to the following concerns raised by fellow faculty members:

1. Unbliblical dualism. Faculty had the impression that everything was understood to have a supernatural cause.

2. Exclusivity of views. This probably reflects its pre-critical, practical approach unusual for a higher education course.

3. A magical approach to the miraculous. This reflects the down-to-earth "workshop" way of teaching the miraculous: this is how you "do" miracles.

4. The privatization of experience. For a "mission" course, it seemed too narrow and insular.

2. For details of this see Pratt, "Need for Dialogue," 7–9.

5. Failures to actually heal. The statistics did not seem to sufficiently verify the claims.[3]

Many of the above criticisms were symptomatic of a couple of quite deliberate philosophical and theological commitments. These will be described below before we move on to the methodology of power encounters.

Wimber's Worldview Critique

John Wimber set about to deconstruct Western scientific materialism.[4] With the help of insights from Harry Blanires's *The Christian Mind*, Wimber identifies the most fundamental way to describe the worldview of the West. It is secularism. By this he means: "The assumption of secular minds is that we live in a universe closed off from divine intervention, in which truth is arrived at through empirical means and rational thought."[5] This is in sharp contrast to pre-modern societies that understand variously capricious spirits and deities to be in control, rendering the world an unpredictable[6] but animated and enchanted place.

Two subsets of secularism, for Wimber's purposes, are materialism and rationalism. Materialism is what gives rise to our attachment to predictable, natural laws to explain everything. And our prioritizing of the material, palpable world affects us even as Christians, according to Wimber: "It warps our thinking, softening convictions about the supernatural world of angels and demons, heaven and hell, Christ and antichrist."[7] As for rationalism, this, according to Wimber, is the reason why we are always seeking, "a rational explanation for all experience."[8] Wimber complains that, "Because angels, demons, God, and spiritual gifts like tongues or prophecy cannot be scientifically measured, secularists employ rationalism to explain away the supernatural."[9]

---

3. Patterson, "Cause for Concern," 20. Also Sarles, "Appraisal of the Signs and Wonders Movement," 63.
4. Mainly found in chapter 5 of his *Power Evangelism*.
5. Wimber and Springer, *Power Evangelism*, 77.
6. Ibid., 74–75. See interesting discussion around understandings of cotton growing in Asian cultures.
7. Wimber and Springer, *Power Evangelism*, 78.
8. Ibid.
9. Ibid.

Wimber's Kingdom Theology

The future age, the kingdom of God, has already invaded the present age, the kingdom of Satan. To use an expression of George Ladd's, we live in "the presence of the future."[10] We are between the times, as it were, between the inauguration and the consummation of the kingdom of God.[11]

> Because our sins are forgiven at the cross and our future bodily resurrections are assured through Christ's resurrection, the Holy Spirit can and does break into this age with signs and assurances of the fullness of the kingdom of God yet to come.[12]

Wimber's indebtedness to theologian George Eldon Ladd is clear. In his reference to this present age as the "kingdom of Satan," however, he is clearly going in a more dualistic direction than Ladd.[13] The main thing that Wimber has added to Ladd's theology is the notion that, as subjects of this kingdom, we have the power and authority to invoke the powers of the age to come in the here and now:

> When Jesus had called the Twelve together, *he gave them power and authority* to drive out all demons and to cure all diseases, and he sent them out to preach the kingdom of God and to heal the sick.... Power is the ability, the strength, the might to complete a given task. Authority is the right to use the power of God.[14]

The happy intrusion of the powers of the age to come into this age is no haphazard thing therefore, but can be made to happen, and these moments of in breaking Wimber terms "power encounters."

Wimber and Power Encounters

The key concept of the power encounter is that it is a moment that involves, "combining the proclamation of the gospel with works of power of the

---

10. Ladd, *Presence of the Future*.
11. Wimber and Springer, *Power Evangelism*, 19.
12. Wimber and Springer, *Power Healing*, 167.
13. "In our war with Satan, there are no demilitarised zones." Wimber and Springer, *Power Evangelism*, 23.
14. Ibid., 24.

Holy Spirit."[15] Power encounters are inspired by conflating two things in the ministry of Jesus: proclamation and demonstration:

> There is no difference between the *words* and *works* of Jesus. The *works* have exactly the same message as the *works*. The message and words concentrated on the announcement of the Kingdom of God. The miracles and works show us what the Kingdom is like.[16]

A power encounter is "a clash between the kingdom of God and the kingdom of Satan."[17] Peter Wagner holds to the same concept, defining it as a demonstration that Christ is, ". . . more powerful than the false gods or spirits worshipped or feared by a people group."[18] Power evangelism, therefore, is any evangelism that is "preceded and undergirded by supernatural demonstrations of God's presence."[19]

Wimber illustrates what he means by this through anecdotes in a way that makes the concept crystal clear. For example, he cites a word of knowledge that he himself received from God about a stranger on a plane who was committing adultery with a woman named "Jane," and how if he did not repent God would take his life. This led to a heartfelt repentance in the cocktail bar followed by a confession to his wife who was also then led to faith in Christ.[20] This is an occasion that Wimber would also describe as a "divine appointment." This is "an appointed time in which God reveals himself to an individual or group through spiritual gifts or other supernatural phenomena."[21]

Wimber's teaching took root in the UK very quickly due to his ability to ingratiate himself with leading Anglicans such as David Watson.[22] They found his laid back approach, free of hype, refreshing and accessible and his influence upon Nicky Gumbel and Holy Trinity Brompton proved pivotal.

---

15. Wimber, "Power Evangelism Definitions and Directions," 21. This is the transcript of a paper given by Wimber at the Academic Symposium on Power Evangelism at Fuller Seminary in 1988.

16. Wimber, "Words and Works of Jesus," 6, cited in Sarles, "An Appraisal of the Signs and Wonders Movement," 73.

17. Sarles, "An Appraisal of the Signs and Wonders Movement," 77.

18. Wagner, "Special Kinds of Church Growth," class notes cited by Wimber and Springer, *Power Evangelism*, 29.

19. Wimber and Springer, *Power Evangelism*, 46.

20. Ibid., 44–46.

21. Ibid., 61.

22. Nigel Scotland tells the story in "From the 'Not Yet' to the 'Now and Not Yet,'" 282.

Evaluation

Responses to Wimber were widely varied, and there was even less of the time lag that previous new phases in the Charismatic tradition enjoyed before the critiques started pouring forth in their now customary abundance. Of these, one study arrived relatively late on the scene—1996—which was arguably the most penetrating. This study was the result Martyn Percy's PhD with King's College, London, published as *Words, Wonders and Power*.[23] In this study Percy studies Wimber and Vineyard as an example of "Fundamentalism." His aims chime with my own aims in this book: "Too many works," he claims, "address the surface or expressive aspects of the tradition, critiquing the symptoms, but not attempting to locate the cause."[24] His use of the word "Fundamentalism" to describe all forms of Christianity that are not liberal, Catholic, or Orthodox is offensive but only in the wake of the way the term has been used post- 9/11 which he could know nothing of at the time. However, his use of "symptoms" betrays the fact that Charismatic faith is apparently to be viewed as a disease.

Even on these terms, we never in fact seem to move beyond symptoms but only to an essentializing move by which the disease ends up being named as its symptoms. The type of sign that symptoms function as in diseases is that of cause and effect, not resemblance. Symptoms do not resemble diseases but indicate their presence. Percy seems to assume resemblance. I can explain this as follows. In *Words, Wonders and Power*, he includes a section on Vineyard style worship. Vineyard songs are, apparently all about a stress on "submission to power."[25] This is their "core theology."[26] Then, a year later, he writes the study of worship at Toronto Airport Vineyard that we looked at in my earlier chapter on Charismatic worship. Here, he claims that sublimated eroticism is likely to be the core ideology behind the whole Toronto phenomenon. The modesty and caution he expresses about this thesis seems slightly feigned: the entire content of the article is presented from this viewpoint. He takes what he sees on the surface: lyrics, bodily movements, and makes these serve as core values. In his analysis of Vineyard worship this core theology shifts from power to eroticism according to what he is observing.

23. Percy, *Words, Wonders and Power*.
24. Ibid., 3.
25. Ibid., 66.
26. Ibid.

When it comes to Wimber himself, Percy is convinced that "concepts of power form the basis of Wimber's thought."[27] Then, instead of looking into how Wimber himself might have developed and understood the language of power, Percy goes straight to the social science of Max Weber and cites a passage that attempts to define what having power over others means when resistance is present.[28] Percy thus ends up conflating power with control to the point where even when critiquing Wimber's "over-realized eschatology," his objection to it not the usual one that critics bring, namely that it damages people's faith by raising their expectations too high,[29] but rather that that such an eschatology fails to value the "freedom and respect that God gives to all creatures."[30] It is too forceful, too powerful. He also decides for Wimber that Wimber has a concept of a God who is more interested in "flexing his muscles" in power encounters with the enemy than in loving people. Wimber's miracles are thus more about pressurizing people into faith[31] than loving them.

Percy's analysis of the ministry of Wimber also seems to belie a certain degree of secularity in his own thinking, a worldview of exactly the kind that the Third Wave was seeking to address. There is an anti-supernatural undercurrent to his critique by which he hopes to explain away nearly all of the supposed miraculous signs that took place in Wimber's ministry. He plucks from any secular framework to hand such as the thought that it might all be to do with the release of endorphins. He ends up with: "What then seems like a miracle to one, is, to another, a complex psychosomatic response to external and internal factors that are somewhat intangible."[32]

A couple of things, however, are useful about Percy's observations. While he seems to have managed to wrongly recast John Wimber as a megalomaniac he has noted a tendency within Charismatic faith to react to Modernity in a frightened way that produces strategies that are basically about control. This would certainly be true of the middle three theologies that we looked at: Shepherding, Word of Faith and Spiritual Warfare. Where Charismatics have given themselves over to a desire for control, Percy is quite correct, there is indeed ". . . a quest for agents that will deliver certainty and

27. Ibid., 18.
28. Ibid., 19, citing Weber, *Theory of Social and Economc Organization*, 152–57.
29. Though he makes this point as well: Percy, *Words, Wonders and Power*, 146.
30. Ibid., 111
31. Ibid., 165.
32. Ibid., 149.

control. . ."[33] Those agents must then show that they have the anointing of God upon them. They must be certain and in control. The pressure of such expectations must surely have been one of the main things that has contributed to the fall from grace of many high profile ministries. However, in fairness to Wimber, one of the most striking marks of his ministry for those who attended his conferences[34] was not only how unassuming and laid back he was as a person but how he began the now widespread move towards "body ministry," or "corporate anointing." Instead of the traditional "healing line" he would invite those who stood near to minister to the sick. The Signs and Wonders doctrine seems relatively free of the urge to control anything, whether people, spiritual forces and laws or territorial spirits.

The second useful observation that Percy made in 1996 was the insularity of the Vineyard and Signs and Wonders movement:

> The type of faith that operates within fundamentalist or charismatic Christian communities is essentially private in nature. What is valued most is the experience of the individual, which authenticates the inductive strategy, and affirms the faith of [the] community.[35]

For all the critique of secular modernity that Wimber's theology brought it did not deal with the secular privatization of religion robustly enough. One of the criticisms of the *Signs and Wonders and Church Growth* course you may recall was that despite being a "Mission Course" there was little that was very outward-facing about it in practice. What we are about to look at is the second generation of the Signs and Wonders movement. While this second generation does not entirely free itself from being a faith authenticating mechanism for believers, it shows real promise as an approach to mission, as I have indicated in my previous chapter. To this we now turn.

---

33. Ibid., 166.

34. In the course of lecturing at Cliff College I have spoken with a number of MA students who were part of the Methodist Charismatic Renewal under Rob Frost: the Easter People. They all attended the early Wimber gatherings and have enthusiastically described them to me. I was only 12 and not a Christian when Wimber first came to Britain so I am grateful for my students filling me in like this.

35. Percy, *Words, Wonders and Power*, 145.

Phase 2: The Rise and Rise of Bill Johnson

A Brief History of Bill Johnson and Bethel

Bill Johnson was born of Earl Johnson who was the pastor of Bethel Church, Redding, at that time an Assemblies of God church. In 1987, Bill Johnson was impacted by the ministry of John Wimber, and then in 1995 by the Toronto Blessing at Toronto Airport Vineyard Church.[36] In 1996, Bill and Brenda (Beni) Johnson become the new pastors of Bethel. The church went from strength to strength, with Bethel Sozo being launched in 1998 and Jesus Culture in 1999, who brought out their first CD in 2006 and pioneered their own church plant in 2013.

In 2006 Bethel Church left AG to become independent and was clearly aligned with the Third Wave teachings of Wimber and Wagner. By 2007 membership had reached 1,500, with a school of supernatural ministry of 1,200 students.[37] In 2011 the Revival Alliance was founded.[38]

There has been an on-going interest in preaching the word "with signs following," and this has tended to be in the tradition of Wimber, including critiques of worldview:

> Marvel is what happens when worldviews fall. Worldviews are people's belief systems—what they believe is possible or not. We have seen people who say that they are agnostic, that they don't believe in God, but then we catch an initiative about them and all of a sudden they get goose bumps and are scared or in awe because it doesn't fit their worldview.[39]

There has also been a continuing interest in the heaven-on-earth, Kingdom of God concept, though the language used is more about now, with not so much a dichotomy between future and present as between heavenly and earthly:

> The wonderful gift from God is the initial earthly manifestation of what exists in his kingdom. It is a testimony of an invisible realm

---

36. He tells his own story in Johnson and Clark, *Essential Guide to Healing*, 35–52.

37. The figure for 2012–13 was 1,800 students: http://bssm.net/about/mission

38 http://supranatural-life.com/Articles/276909/Supranatural_Life/Events/Revival_Alliance_Gathering.aspx. This consists of six international ministries: Bill and Beni Johnson, Randy and DeAnne Clark, Georgian and Winnie Banov, Che and Sue Ahn, Roland and Heidi Baker, and John and Carol Arnott: http://revivalalliance.com/

39. Walker, *Catching the Initiatives of Heaven*, 34.

called the Kingdom of God. Through prayer we are able to pull that reality into this one . . . [40]

The kingdom concept at Bethel also seems to have moved from an inaugurated eschatology breaking through in power encounters to a realized eschatology waiting for us to recognize its present availability:

> It's no longer a question of heaven or hell. It's only a question of how much of hell's thinking I will allow into this heavenly mind of mine. Doesn't it honor Him more when His children no longer see themselves as *sinners saved by grace*, but now as *heirs of God*?[41]

> Some people teach that the Kingdom of God is for some time in the distant future or past, not here and now. . . . But Jesus taught and demonstrated that the kingdom of God is a present-tense reality—it exists now in the invisible realm.[42]

Shuttleworth has rightly dubbed this a shift from a "now and not yet" eschatology (which Wimber drew from Ladd) to a "now and mystery" eschatology.[43] In other words, he is so uncomfortable with affirming anything that might be a mere promise and not realizable as a present actuality that, instead of explaining divine non-interventions by reference to an as yet imperfectly realized future age, he relegates them to "mystery":

> I teach our people that if now, but not yet is used to define promise and potential, accept it. If it is spoken to build awareness of our limitations and restrictions, reject it.[44]

Johnson's eschatology seems, at the very least, to teeter on the brink between an inaugurated and a realized one. Some would doubtless say it is already over-realized. Bell insists, however, that Johnson's kingdom theology merely takes Wimber's kingdom theology to its logical conclusion and, as such, is actually more consistent with itself.[45] After all, both Wimber and Johnson claimed Jesus as their ultimate model. For Johnson this means that the standard is a perfect track record: everyone that came

---

40. Johnson, *When Heaven Invades Earth*, 46.
41. Johnson and Mills, *Supernatural Power of a Transformed Mind*, 149.
42. Ibid., 41.
43. Shuttleworth, "Critical Discussion," 112.
44. Johnson, *Dreaming with God*, 65.
45. Bell, "Does the Theology of Healing," 12.

to him was healed.[46] The only wriggle room is Mark 9:28 where it is clear that some pressing in or pursuit was needed. The blind man's sight was not completely restored the first time Jesus ministered to him. In fact this passage is a precedent within the movement for the style of ministry employed. The method is to lay hands on the person and minister healing to them and then ask how the person feels. If the person is not healed but has sensed something happening, this helps to spur on the ministry team to pray again, and indeed to repeat the process for as long as seems necessary. For Wimber, sick people not recovering after prayer ministry could be put down to the fact that in an already-not yet kingdom, not everyone is going to be healed in this life. For Johnson, the failure to be healed is a signal to make more of a "demand" upon one's faith, to take a bigger risk perhaps, to press in rather than pull back.[47] So, Bell would insist that there does remain a not-yet element to Johnson's kingdom theology, it is an inaugurated and not a realized eschatology,[48] but it is the Mark 9:28 kind of not-yet: the not yet of the prayerful and expectant pusuit of God's will until it is done on earth as it is in heaven.

Bill Johnson's ministry has spawned a profusion of imitations and a multiplicity of American dominated conferences that teach eager listeners about how to be "naturally supernatural." The emphasis, as with Wimber, is with the "corporate Anointing." There is an avowed disengagement from the classic Kathryn Khulman or Benny Hinn model of superstar stage-strutting theatrics in favor of getting members of the congregation to, in a suitably charged atmosphere, lay hands on one another for healing and miracles. Johnson himself never raises his voice on stage and delivers most of his messages with his hands in his pockets.

Conclusion

Indulge me for a moment in some silliness. As I am in the middle of marking season at Cliff College at the moment, I have come up with a brilliant way of assessing the five theologies we have looked at. If the five innovations were undergraduate essays I would give the Inner Healing paper, as it were, a mark in the B category. In the British system it would get a mark

---

46. Johnson, "Is it Always God's Will to Heal Someone?" http://bjm.org/qa/is-it-always-gods-will-to-heal-someone/.

47. Johnson, "Weaverville," http://bjm.org/bill/.

48. Bell, "Does the Theology of Healing," 12–13.

in the lower 60s, a 2:1. This is because, overall, it works as an authentically Christian expression of faith, retrieving aspects of that faith's therapeutic roots. What it still needs is a yet stronger theoretical basis that could both deepen its biblical authenticity and strengthen the credibility of its interactions with psychology and (more recently) neurology. But there must be a decidedly biblical-theological bias so that secular ideas are truly woven into Christianity, not vice-versa.

I would give the Shepherding Movement a grade in the 40s, a D, as some issues have been clearly understood and the importance of discipleship identified in a prescient way, yet the execution, namely the bolstering of religious authority rather than the facilitating of better discipleship, was deeply flawed.

I would give Word of Faith a grade in the 30s; an E (or F in the American system). It is a fail because it has failed to communicate a genuinely Christian concept of faith but has sold people something else which seems to answer their deepest fears and needs, but has failed to be honest about the true nature of the product.

Spiritual Warfare is to be praised for its critique of the Western worldview. However, it proceeds to make similar mistakes to Word of Faith. It tries to answer people's fears about a world out of control and offers the power to wrest back control at the expense of a genuinely Christ-centered faith. This gets a grade in the 40s at best: a D.

However, what we find in Signs and Wonders teaching is far more promising. As a movement it is prone to the same faddishness, the same excess of prophetic certitude and the same monotonous concentration on a single issue that the other movements within the Charismatic movement display. And despite its professed repudiation of hype and showmanship, there is a lingering showiness to the on-stage presence of Revival Alliance preachers. Yet Signs and Wonders can boast three things that the other four display only in part:

1. Its theology is authentically Christian, basing itself on the Kingdom teachings of Jesus. It is aided by much the same worldview critique as Spiritual Warfare but is not dominated by animistic techniques.
2. It has an academic underpinning supplied by George Eldon Ladd and Paul Hiebert. These names are more than a badge of legitimation but genuinely informed the thinking of Wimber (whether they wanted to or not).

3. It is creatively, sensitively and authentically applied, and not only towards helping Christians to get more blessed but towards reaching out in acts of kindness to the world.

Signs and Wonders, then, retains the compassionate approach to secular culture that Inner Healing brought, spurning the angrier reactions of Shepherding, Word of Faith and Spiritual Warfare. It exercises faith after the bold manner of Word of Faith advocates but with only a fraction of the less helpful Word of Faith baggage. It retains and builds on the worldview critique of Spiritual Warfare but arrives at somewhat softer outcomes.

It is almost as though the Charismatic movement's first thought in the midst of rapid liberalizing and secularizing cultural change was a good one—to reach out a hand of healing to troubled people. Then, as the world became even scarier, its second, third and fourth thoughts were an overly negative response which failed to reach out in an authentically Christian way to the world. Finally, with Wimber, something starts to take shape that utilizes the best of the insights from the previous thoughts, and which is then developed by Johnson and his followers into a missiological tactic.

It seems to me that a worldwide Church that takes some cues from the first and fifth innovations will be a healing Church, a dynamic Church, an authentic Church, a Church which will be respected even by the masses of those who dare not join (Acts 5:13). Conversely, to adopt the middle three: Shepherding, Faith and Warfare, would be to subscribe to a faith for control-freaks. Christians need never and should never lay claim to the level of control over people and over spiritual forces and laws that those three theologies encourage.

Conclusion

I have hopefully demonstrated that Western Pentecostalism is not one thing but three distinct things. In saying this, I have claimed nothing new but have merely reaffirmed the division into into Classical Pentecostalism, Charismatic Renewal and Neo-Charismatic networks. But what I have added is to say that even these last two things can be further divided into five. I have shown that, once stripped of distinctives that are more properly native to Classical Pentecostalism, and once further divided into five distinct units of thought and practice, Charismatic Christianity becomes much easier to assess. We then have the power to neither write off the movement nor uncritically acquiesce but can choose what we want to take and develop within our own traditions, and what we would rather leave behind.

These five components can also be reassembled to demonstrate the features they share, which hopefully helps us see the entire Charismatic project as a critique, in various forms, of late modernity. This, in turn, helps us to see where it finds common cause with other perhaps more sophisticated movements within Christian theology and ministry such as Radical Orthodoxy or Whole Life Discipleship, which might add some better theoretical underpinning.

At their worst, what these teachings tend to offer is the possibility of extraordinarily high levels of insight into, and control over, the universe. Subscribers need no longer fear the way life seems so frighteningly free, so out of control. Now, all is explained, everything is clear and brought under control. It is the old existential angst of Sartre showing itself in Western spirituality. And this spirituality is not anti-Christian or un-Christian, but it is para-Christian. It is Christanimism.

However, this is not the whole story, and too many critics have stopped here. Alongside this tendency towards animistic control is an entirely different urge. There are thus two urgencies that run through the most distinctive innovations of Charismatic faith, both of which are part of its critique of late modernity: one a negative response, and the other a positive one. Besides the urge towards control there is also the urge towards authenticity. The controlling tendencies were at their worst during the political and moral turmoil of the sixties and seventies when governments were throwing their legislative weight behind rampant liberalism, and produced Christanimism. The urge towards authenticity, however, is to be welcomed. Charismatic Christianity has been at its best when compassion, rather than control, takes prime position. Charismatics are then able to express their exasperation with secular modernity in constructive and outward-looking ways, ways that try to bring healing to the whole person, ways that are Christ-like, and early church-like.

The task for Charismatics, then, is to tease out the one strand from the other. The urge to control needs to find its answer in a much bigger God-concept, perhaps drawing from the well of the Reformational traditions with their high view of the sovereignty of God. As a Charismatic I can still recall my first encounters with Louis Berkhof's definitions of the attributes of God. These made me worship God and find refuge in a God who was more than enough, which was an antidote to a church life dominated by insatiable cries for more of God's Spirit, more of his miracles, more, more, more. Terry Virgo, to his great credit, is one of very few Charismatic leaders to have seriously engaged with the Reformed tradition. He takes genuine delight in such things as John Murray's commentary on Romans, and writes with wisdom about the subject of God's sovereign grace.[1]

Charismatics should also build on their particular style of authenticity by drawing water from the wells of the Eastern Orthodox tradition with its profoundly therapeutic soteriology centered on deification[2]—a concept that Word of Faith teaching has already articulated in its own rather flawed way. Irenaeus, Athanasius and the Cappadocian Fathers proclaimed the healing of the human race via the descent into humanity of God himself and the subsequent lifting of humanity into becoming partakers of the divine nature. Charismatics would doubtless find that they *do* have a use for the kind of atonement espoused by these patristic authors. The Orthodox also have a strong pneumatology and a model of the Trinity that does not subordinate the Spirit in the same way that the Western model does.

---

1. See his *God's Lavish Grace* and *Enjoying God's Grace*, and also his autobiographical *No Well-Worn Paths*.

2. Beautifully outlined in Lossky, *Mystical Theology of the Eastern Church*.

Conclusion

Some Charismatic leaders, most notably Michael Harper, did go over to the Orthodox faith, and it is easy to see why.

I wonder if our search for a genuinely *post*-modern and *post*-secular Christianity ought to have begun with the Charismatics all along. John Drane looked for a sufficiently affective form of Christianity and despaired that postmodern people do not even consider Christianity as an option because it is not spiritual enough. For reasons that were not clear, the possibility that Charismatic ways of being church might be part of the answer to this problem was not countenanced, which somewhat baffled me as a Charismatic church-goer at the time of his *Cultural Change and Biblical Faith*. Church for me was a highly numinous and senuous experience. He seemed to write as though Pentecostalism did not exist. Brian McLaren sees Charismatic Christianity as simply part of the problem. All forms of Christianity, for him, are hopelessly wedded to modernity, which, as I hope this book has made clear, is clearly not the case. Charismatic faith, like its Pentecostal ancestor, has been boldly trying to take on the assumptions of modernity from the start.

Lastly, a word on syncretism is probably in order. Charismatic Christianity has been unblushingly syncretistic of seemingly anything at all that helps in the quest for more power to make a difference in secular culture. This is where it could learn from Radical Orthodoxy. I read Milbank, Pickstock, Ward and Smith for their attitude. I find that their attitude towards the air of legitimacy that our secular culture wears is a breath of fresh air. Too often, Charismatic faith, steels this and that from the culture and then retreats into its ghetto to develop new syncretisms in private. It is at its best when it stays out in the open and does its healing on the streets. The RO attitude will help with that. RO could also supply some wisdom about how to syncretize in the right way. Here is Milbank: ". . . just as Irenaeus learned much from Valentinus, the distortions develop better certain aspects of orthodoxy which orthodoxy must then later recoup."[3] His insight is that secularity is a faith position which, for its creed, has often taken various aspects of Christian faith and either distorted them or developed them. As Milbank has shown, in the hands of secular culture, some of these Christian doctrines have actually got better and more useful. They have kept better pace with changes in science and culture. These should be woven back into the faith. An example that I am working on is addiction recovery programs. The very concept of a program for dealing with addictions is of

---

3. Milbank, *Theology and Social Theory*, xv.

deeply Christian origins but, since the 1980s, has developed in non-faith directions with some programs such as Rational Recovery having developed precisely because of an angry attitude towards the more faith-based 12-step approach. To my delight I have found that both the faith-based (but frankly out-of-date) approaches and the anti-faith approaches have resonances with Christian faith, especially Pauline theology, which can very readily be re-integrated. It is a perfect example of what Milbank describes. My task is to make sure that what I end up with is genuinely rooted in Christian faith and not just an eclectic mess.

So, while critiquing Charismatic practice has slid out of intellectual fashion, the task of treating Charismatic theology as a serious contribution to Christian thought has only just begun. My prayer is that my efforts will get to where they can be proved the most useful and stimulate further research and experiments in ministry. There is a great deal to learn from the mistakes and successes of Charismatic faith about what a post-secular, compassion-driven, healing Church could look like. The healing Church may well not resemble the Charismatic church of today but will have heard its voice, learned its lessons, and applied its insights.

Bibliography

Aldis, W. H. *The Message of Keswick and its Meaning.* London: Marshall, Morgan & Scott, n.d.
Algera, J. A. *Signs and Wonders of God's Kingdom.* Philadelphia, PA: Westminster Theological Seminary, 1993.
Anane-Asane, A., et al. "Paul Hiebert's 'The Flaw of the Excluded Middle.'" *Trinity Journal* 30 (2009) 189–97.
Anderson N., and S. Goss. *Freedom in Christ.* Oxford: Monarch, 2009.
Anderson, A. *An Introduction to Pentecostalism: Global Charismatic Christianity.* Cambridge: Cambridge University Press, 2004.
Anderson, D. "Idealism in American Thought." In *The Blackwell Guide to American Philosophy,* edited by A. Marsobian and J. Ryder, 22–34. Oxford: Blackwell, 2004.
Anderson, N. *The Bondage Breaker: Overcoming Negative Thoughts, Irrational Feelings and Habitual Sin.* Guildford: Monarch, 1996.
———. *Steps to Freedom in Christ.* Oxford: Monarch, 2009.
Anderson, R. M. *Vision of the Disinherited: The Making of American Pentecostalism.* Oxford: University Press, 1979.
Anon. "The Conference in Germany." *Confidence* 2.1 (Jan. 1909) 6.
———. "Faith in His Blood." *Confidence* 4.8 (August 1911) 188.
Armstrong, K. *Fields of Blood: Religion and the History of Violence.* London: Bodley Head, 2014.
Armstrong, T. "South Africa." *Confidence* 1.9 (Dec. 1908) 20.
Arnold, C. *3 Crucial Questions about Spiritual Warfare.* Grand Rapids: Baker 1997.
Atkinson, W. *The Death of Jesus: A Pentecostal Investigation.* Leiden: Brill, 2009.
———. "The Nature of the Crucified Christ in Word-Faith Teaching." *Evangelical Review of Theology* 31.2 (2007) 169–84.
———. "A Theological Appraisal of the Doctrine that Jesus Died Spiritually, as Taught by Kenyon, Hagin and Copeland." PhD diss., Edinburgh University, 2007.
Ayegboyin, D. I. "A Rethinking of Prosperity Teaching in the New Pentecostal Churches in Nigeria." *Black Theology* 4.1 (2006) 70–86.
Baker, H., and S. Pradhan, *Compelled by Love.* Lake Mary, FL: Charisma, 2008.
Basham, D. *A Handbook on Holy Spirit Baptism.* Monroeville, PA: Whitaker, 1969.
Baughen, M., ed. *Youth Praise Book One.* London: Falcon, 1966.
Bebbington, D. "The Advent Hope in British Evangelicalism since 1800." *Scottish Journal of Religious Studies* 9.2 (1988) 103–114.

———. "Evangelicals and Public Worship 1965–2005." *Evangelical Quarterly* 79.1 (2007) 3–21.

———. *Evangelicalism in Modern Britain: A History from 1730s to the 1980s*. London: Unwin, 1989.

———. *Holiness in Nineteenth Century Britain*. Carlisle: Paternoster, 2000.

Begbie, J. *Theology, Music and Time*. Cambridge: Cambridge University Press, 2000.

Begunder, M. "The Cultural Turn." In *Studying Global Pentecostalism: Theories and Methods*, edited by Allan Anderson et al., 52–56. Los Angeles: University of California Press, 2010.

Bell, J. "Does the Theology of Healing as Presented by Bill Johnson and his Key Influences Represent a Biblical Model of Healing?" BA diss., University of Manchester, 2016.

Bennett, D. *Nine O'Clock in the Morning*. Plainfield: Bridge, 1970.

Bentley, T. *The Journey into the Miraculous*. Shippensburg, PA: Destiny Image, 2008.

Biblical Discernment Ministries, "Paul (David) Yonggi Cho: General Teachings/Activities." Online: http://www.rapidnet.com/~jbeard/bdm/exposes/cho/general.htm.

Bobgan, M., and D. Bobgan. *TheoPhostic Counseling: Divine Revelation or PsychoHeresy?* Santa Barbara, CA: Eastgate, 1999.

Boddy, A. "An Apostolic Welsh Revival." *Confidence* 6.2 (1913) 28.

———. "Divine Necrosis: Or the Deadness of the Lord Jesus." *Confidence* 1.9 (Dec. 1908) 3–7.

Boddy, M. "Life out of Death." *Confidence* 5.4 (1912) 110.

Bokovay, K. W. "The Relationship of Physical Healing to the Atonement." *Didaskalia* 3.2 (1991) 26–35.

Bolt, C., and A. R. Lee. *Introduction to American Studies*. London: Longman, 1981.

Bond, K. M. *Signs and Wonders: Perspectives on John Wimber's Vineyard*. Langley, BC: Northwest Baptist Theological Seminary, 1990.

Booker, M., and M. Ireland. *Evangelism: Which Way Now. An Evaluation of Alpha, Emmaus, Cell Church and other Contemporary Strategies for Evangelism*. London: Church, 2005.

Bosworth, F. F. *Christ the Healer*. Old Tappan, NJ: Revell, 1973.

Boustan, R., et al., eds. *Violence, Scripture, and Textual Practice in Early Judaism and Christianity*. Leiden: Brill, 2009.

Bowater, C. *A Believer's Guide to Worship*. Eastbourne: Kingsway, 1986.

Boyd, G. *God at War: The Bible and Spiritual Conflict*. Downers Grove, IL: InterVarsity, 1997.

Braden, C. S. *Spirits in Rebellion: The Rise and Development of New Thought*. Dallas: Southern Methodist University Press, 1963.

Brian, S. "Researching Alpha" *Journal of Adult Theological Education* 3.1 (2006) 75–85.

Bridge, D. *Power Evangelism and the Word of God*. Eastbourne: Kingsway, 1987.

Brookes, A., ed. *The Alpha Phenomenon*. London: Churches Together in Britain and Ireland, 2007.

Buell, L., ed. *The American Transcendentalists: Essential Writings*. New York: The Modern Library, 2006.

Bulle, F. *God Wants You Rich and Other Enticing Doctrines*. Minneapolis, MN: Bethany, 1983.

Camp, L. *Mere Discipleship: Radical Christianity in a Rebellious World*. Grand Rapids: Brazos, 2003.

Bibliography

Capon, John. *And There Was Light: Story of the Nationwide Festival of Light.* London: Lutterworth, 1972.

Capps, C. *The Tongue: A Creative Force.* Tulsa: Harrison, 1976.

Carlson, C. "The Roots of Christian Zionism: How Scofield Sowed Seeds of Apostasy." Online: https://www.youtube.com/watch?v=IO6VpMYAVms.

Carr, W. *Angels and Principalities.* Cambridge University Press, 1981.

Carson, D. A. "God, the Bible and Spiritual Warfare: A Review Article." *Journal of the Evangelical Theological Society* 42.2 (1999) 251–69.

Cartledge, M. "The Early Pentecostal Theology of Confidence Magazine (1908–1926): A Version of the Five-Fold Gospel?" *Journal of the European Pentecostal Theological Association* 28.2 (2008) 117–30.

Cavanaugh, W. "'A Fire Strong Enough to Consume the House:' The Wars of Religion and the Rise of the State." *Modern Theology* 11.4 (1995) 397–420.

Chant, B. *Heart of Fire.* Adelaide: House of Tabor, 1984.

Christian Discernment. "Theophostic Theology: God's Light or Darkness?" Online: http://www.christiandiscernment.com/Christian%20Discernment/CD%20PDF/Book%20pdf/31%20Theophostic%20Theology%20FINAL%20PAPER.pdf.

Clifton, S. *Pentecostal Churches in Transition: Analysing the Developing Ecclesiology of the Assemblies of God in Australia.* Leiden: Brill, 2009.

Collins, J. *Exorcism and Deliverance Ministry in the Twentieth Century: An Analysis of the Practice of Exorcism in Modern Western Christianity.* Milton Keynes: Paternoster, 2009.

Cooper, J. *Glory in the Church.* Milton Keynes: Authentic, 1996.

Copan, P., and M. Flannagan. *Did God Really Command Genocide? Coming to Terms with the Justice of God.* Grand Rapids: Baker, 2014.

Copeland, K. *The Decision is Yours.* Fort Worth: Kenneth Copeland, 1998.

———. *The Force of Faith.* Fort Worth: Kenneth Copeland, 1983.

———. *Giving and Receiving.* Fort Worth: Kenneth Copeland, 1985.

———. *The Laws of Prosperity.* Fort Worth: Kenneth Copeland, 1974.

———. *The Power of the Tongue.* Fort Worth: Kenneth Copeland, 1980.

———. *Walking in the Realm of the Miraculous.* Fort Worth: Kenneth Copeland, 1980.

Cornwall, J. *Let us Praise.* South Plainfield, NJ: Bridge, 1973.

Corsini, R., and A. Auerbach, eds. *Concise Encyclopedia of Psychology.* 2nd ed. New York: John Wiley, 1998.

Cotterell, T., and N. Hudson. *Leading a Whole-Life Disciplemaking Church.* Cambridge: Grove, 2012.

Cowles, C. S. *Show Them No Mercy: 4 Views on God and Canaanite Genocide.* Grand Rapids: Zondervan, 2003.

Cox, H. *Fire from Heaven: The Rise of Pentecostal Spirituality and the Reshaping of Religion in the Twenty-First Century.* London: Cassell, 1996.

Cunningham, R. J. "From Holiness to Healing: Faith Cure in America 1872–1892." *Church History* 43.3 (1974) 499–513.

Da Silva, A. B. "The 'Theology of Success' Movement: A Comment." *Themelios* 11.3 (1986) 91–2.

Dawson, J. *Taking our Cities for God.* Lake Mary, FL: Creation, 1989.

Dayton, D. "The Rise of the Evangelical Healing Movement in 19th Century America." *Pneuma* 4.1 (1982) 1–18.

Dayton, D. *Theological Roots of Pentecostalism.* London: Scarecrow, 1987.

BIBLIOGRAPHY

De Certeau, M. *The Practice of Everyday Life*. Translated by. S. Rendall. Berkeley, CA: University of California Press, 1984.

De Jong, Mary G. "'I Want to be Like Jesus': The Self-Defining Power of Evangelical Hymnody." *Journal of the American Academy of Religion* 54.3 (1986) 461–93.

Dearmer, P., and R.Vaughan Williams, eds. *The English Hymnal*. London: Oxford University Press, 1906.

DeArteaga, W. *Quenching the Spirit: Examining Centuries of Opposition to the Moving of the Holy Spirit*. Altamonte Springs: Creation, 1992.

DeBernardi, J. "Spiritual Warfare and Territorial Spirits: The Globalization and Localisation of a 'Practical Theology.'" *Religious Studies and Theology* 18.2 (1999) 66–96.

Dedmon, K. *The Ultimate Treasure Hunt: A Guide to Supernatural Evangelism*. Shippensburg: Destiny Image, 2007.

Deere, J. *Surprised by the Power of the Spirit*. Eastbourne: Kingsway, 1993.

Dineen, T. *Manufacturing Victims: What the Psychology Industry is Doing to People*. Second Edition. Montreal: Robert Davies Multimedia, 1998.

Doyle, R., et al. *Signs & Wonders and Evangelicals: A Response to the Teaching of John Wimber*. Sydney: Lancer, 1987.

Drane, John. *Cultural Change and Biblical Faith*. Carlisle: Paternoster, 2000.

Dresser, H. W., ed. *The Quimby Manuscripts*. New York: Thomas Y. Crowell, 1921.

Dunn, J. *Baptism in the Holy Spirit*. London: SCM, 1970.

Dyer, A. "Some Theological Trends Reflected in the Songs used by the British Charismatic Churches of 1970s to Early 2000s." *Journal of the European Pentecostal Theological Association* 26.1 (2006) 36–48.

Elder Cumming, J. "What We Teach." In *Keswick's Triumphant Voice*, edited by H. F. Stevenson, 17–25. London: Marshall, Morgan & Scott, 1963.

Ellis, A., and C. MacLaren, *Rational Emotive Behavior Therapy: A Therapist's Guide*. Atascadero, CA: Impact, 2005.

Ellis, B. *Raising the Devil: Satanism, New Religious Movements, and the Media*. Lexington, KY: University Press of Kentucky, 2000.

Entwistle, D. "Shedding Light on Theophostic Ministry 2: Ethical and Legal Issues." *Journal of Psychology and Theology* 32.1 (2004) 35–42.

Epictetus, *Enchiridion*. Translated by R. Dobbin. London: Penguin, 2008.

Evans, E. *The Welsh Revival of 1904*. Bridgend: Evangelical Press of Wales, 1969.

Faupel, D.W. *The Everlasting Gospel: The Significance of Eschatology in the Development of Pentecostal Thought*. Sheffield Academic Press, 1996.

Fee, G., *Gospel and Spirit: Issues in New Testament Hermeneutics*. Peabody: Hendrickson, 1991.

Flood, D. *Healing the Gospel: A Radical Vision for Grace, Justice, and the Cross*. Eugene, OR: Cascade, 2012.

Forwell, G., trans. *Zinzendorf: Nine Public Lectures on Important Subjects in Religion*. Iowa City: University of Iowa Press, 1973.

Frothingham, O. B. *Transcendentalism in New England: A History*. New York: Harper, 1959.

Frykholm, Amy. "Calculated Blessings: A Visit to John Hagee's Church." *Christian Century* (October 7, 2008) 35–37.

Garrard, M. *Mrs Penn-Lewis: A Memoir*. Westbourne: Overcomer Book Room, 1947.

Garzon, F. et al, "Freedom in Christ: Quasi-Experimental Research on the Neil Anderson Approach." *Journal of Psychology and Theology* 29.1 (2001) 41–51.

Bibliography

Gee, D. *Concerning Spiritual Gifts.* Springfield, MO: Gospel Publishing, 1949.
General Synod. *The Charismatic Movement in the Church of England.* London: Church House, 1981.
Glass, J. "Eschatology: A Clear and Present Danger—A Sure and Certain Hope." In *Pentecostal Perspectives,* edited by Keith Warrington, 120–46. Carlisle: Paternoster, 1998.
Goff, J. R. "The Faith That Claims." *Christianity Today* (February 19, 1990) 18–19.
Goheen, M. "The Lasting Legacy of Lesslie Newbigin." *Q Ideas.* Online: http://qideas.org/articles/the-lasting-legacy-of-lesslie-newbigin/.
Goodiff, A. "'It's all About Jesus': A Critical Analysis of the Ways in which the Songs of Four Contemporary Worship Christian Songwriters can Lead to an Impoverished Christology." *Evangelical Quarterly* 81.3 (2009) 254–68.
Gordon, A. J. *The Ministry of Healing.* In *Healing: The Three Great Healing Classics,* edited by J. Graf. Camp Hill, PA: Christian Publications, 1992.
Graf, J., ed. *Healing: The Three Great Classics on Divine Healing.* Camp Hill: Christian Publications, 1992.
Granberg, S. "Christianity with Power, by Charles H. Kraft." *Restoration Quarterly* 34 (1992) 190–91.
Greene, Mark. *The Great Divide.* London: LICC, 2010.
Greenlee, D. 'Territorial Spirits Reconsidered." *Missiology: An International Review* 22.4 (1994) 507–14.
Guelich, R. "Spiritual Warfare: Jesus, Paul and Peretti." *The Journal of the Society for Pentecostal Studies* 2.1 (1991) 33–64.
Gumprecht, J. *Abusing Memory: The Healing Theology of Agnes Sanford.* Moscow, ID: Canon, 2010.
Gura, P. *American Transcendentalism: A History.* New York: Hill & Wang, 2007.
Hagin, K. *The Authority of the Believer.* Tulsa: Faith Library, 1980.
———. *Bible Faith Study Course.* Tulsa: Faith Library, 1974.
———. *How to Turn Your Faith Loose.* 2nd ed. Tulsa: Faith Library, 1983.
———. *In Him.* Tulsa: Faith Library, 1979.
———. *Learning to Flow With the Spirit of God.* Tulsa: Faith Library, 1986.
———. *New Thresholds of Faith.* Tulsa: faith Library, 1985.
———. *Observations on Fasting.* Tulsa: Faith Library, n.d.
———. *Prayer Secrets.* Tulsa: Faith Library, 1967.
———. *The Real Faith.* Tulsa: Faith Library, 1980.
———. *Right and Wrong Thinking.* Tulsa: Faith Library, 1986.
———. *Three Big Words.* Tulsa: Faith Library, 1983.
———. *What Faith Is.* 2nd Ed. Tulsa: Faith Library, 1983.
———. *Why Do People Fall Under the Power?* Tulsa: Faith Library, 1983.
———. *Words.* Tulsa: Faith Library, 1979.
———. *You Can Have What You Say.* Tulsa: Faith Library, 1979.
———. *Your Faith in God Will Work.* Tulsa: Faith Library, 1991.
———. *Zoe: The God-Kind of Life.* Tulsa: Faith Library, 1983.
Hammond, F., and I. M. Hammond. *Pigs in the Parlor: A Practical Guide to Deliverance.* Kirkwood, MO: Impact, 1973.
Hand, C. *Falling Short? The Alpha Course Examined.* Epsom: DayOne, 1998.
Hanegraaff, H. *Christianity in Crisis.* Eugene: Harvest, 1997.
Harper, M. *Spiritual Warfare.* London: Hodder & Stoughton, 1970.

BIBLIOGRAPHY

Harrison, A. "'There Must be More Than This': Current Dilemmas Concerning Congregational Song," *Anvil* 23.4 (2006) 275–86.

Harrison, M. *Righteous Riches: The Word of Faith Movement in Contemporary African American Religion.* Oxford: Oxford University Press, 2005.

Hauerwas, S. *Against the Nations: War and Survival in a Liberal Society.* Notre Dame, IN: University of Notre Dame Press, 1992.

Heard, J. *Inside Alpha: Explorations in Evangelism.* Milton Keynes: Paternoster, 2009.

Hewitt, B. *Doing a New Thing.* London: Hodder & Stoughton, 1995.

Hey, S. *Mega Churches: Origins, Ministry and Prospects.* Melbourne: Mosaic, 2013.

Hiebert, P. *Anthropological Reflections on Missiological Issues.* Grand Rapids: Baker, 1994.

———. "The Flaw of the Excluded Middle." *Missiology: An International Review* 10.1 (1982) 35–47.

———. "Spiritual Warfare: Biblical Perspectives." *Mission Focus* 20.3 (1992) 41–46.

Hill, C., and M. *And They Shall Prophesy!* London: Marshall Pickering, 1990.

Hio-Kee Ooi, S. "A Study of Strategic-Level Spiritual Warfare from a Chinese Perspective." *Asian Journal of Pentecostal Studies* 9 (2006) 143–61.

Hitchcock, W. *Music in the United States: A Historical Introduction.* Englewood Cliffs, NJ: Prentice-Hall, 1969.

Horn, Nico. "Power and Empowerment in the Political Context of South Africa." *Journal of the European Pentecostal Theological Association* 25 (2005) 7–24.

Horrobin, P. *Healing Through Deliverance.* Chichester: Sovereign World, 1991.

Horton, H. *The Gifts of the Spirit.* Luton: Assemblies of God, 1934.

Hubbard, R. *Isaiah 53: Is There Healing in the Atonement?* Bromley: New Life, 1972.

Hudson, N. *Imagine Church: Releasing Whole-Life Disciples.* Nottingham: IVP, 2012.

Hughes, P. *The Pentecostals in Australia.* Canberra: Australian Government, 1996.

Hughes, P., et al. *Australia's Religious Communities.* Nunawading: Christian Research Association, 2012.

Hunt, D., and T. A. McMahon. *The Seduction of Christianity: Spiritual Discernment in the Last Days.* Eugene, OR: Harvest, 1985.

Hunt, S. "Giving the Devil More than His Due: Some Problems with Deliverance Ministry." In *Harmful Religion: An Exploration of Religious Abuse,* edited by L. Osborn and A. Walker, 54–58. London: SPCK, 1997.

Hunt, S. *The Alpha Enterprise.* Aldershot: Ashgate, 2004.

———. *Anyone for Alpha? Evangelism in a Post-Christian Society.* London: DLT, 2001.

Hunter, H. D. "Shepherding Movement." In *Dictionary of Pentecostal And Charismatic Movements,* edited by Stanley Burgess et al., 784. Grand Rapids: Zondervan, 1990.

Jackson, B. "Stapleton: A Study in Psychotheological Naiveté," *Journal of Psychology and Theology* 8.3 (1980) 195–97.

Jacobs, C. *Possessing the Gates of the Enemy: A Training Manual for Militant Intercession.* Bloomington, MN: 1991.

Jersak, B. and M. Hardin, eds. *Stricken by God? Nonviolent Identification and the Victory of Christ.* Grand Rapids: Eerdmans, 2007.

Johnson, B. *Dreaming with God.* Shippensburg, PA: Destiny Image, 2006.

———. *Hosting the Presence.* Shippensburg, PA: Destiny Image, 2012.

———. "Is it Always God's Will to Heal Someone?" Personal Blog. Online: http://bjm.org/qa/is-it-always-gods-will-to-heal-someone/.

———. *When Heaven Invades Earth.* Shippensburg, PA: Destiny Image, 2003.

Bibliography

Johnson, B., and D. Mills. *The Supernatural Power of a Transformed Mind*. Shippensburg, PA: Destiny Image, 2005.
Johnson, B., and R. Clark. *The Essential Guide to Healing*. Bloomington, MN: Chosen, 2011.
Johnson, D., and J. Van Vonderen. *The Subtle Power of Spiritual Abuse*. Minneapolis: Bethany, 1991.
Jones, B. P. *An Instrument of Revival: The Complete Life of Evan Roberts 1878–1951*. South Plainfield, NJ.: Bridge, 1995.
Judah, J. S. *The History and Philosophy of the Metaphysical Movements in America*. Philadelphia: Westminster, 1967.
Judd-Montgomery, C. "Faith's Reckonings." *Triumphs of Faith* 1 (1881) 2–3.
Kay, W. "A Demonised Worldview: Dangers, Benefits and Explanations." *Journal of Empirical Theology* 11 (1998) 17–29.
———. *Apostolic Networks in Britain: New Ways of Being Church*. Milton Keynes: Paternoster, 2007.
———. "Apostolic Networks in the UK: The Dynamics of Growth." *Journal of the European Pentecostal Theological Association* 25 (2005) 25–38.
———. "Approaches to Healing in British Pentecostalism." *Journal of Pentecostal Theology* 14 (1999) 113–25.
———. *Pentecostalism*. London: SCM, 2009.
Kay, W., and A. Dyer. *Pentecostal and Charismatic Studies: A Reader*. London: SCM, 2004.
Kay, W., and R. Parry, eds. *Exorcism and Deliverance: Multi-Disciplinary Studies*. Milton Keynes: Paternoster, 2011.
Kendrick, G. *Make Way Songbook*. Eastbourne: Kingsway, 1986.
Kenyon, A. "A Testimony from Bracknell." *Confidence* 1.5 (Aug 1908) 9.
Kenyon, E. W. *The Hidden Man: An Unveiling of the Subconscious Mind*. Kenyon's Gospel, 1998.
———. *Identification: A Romance in Redemption*. Kenyon's Gospel, 1998.
———. *In His Presence, The Secret of Prayer*. Kenyon's Gospel, 1993.
———. *The Two Kinds of Faith: Faith's Secrets Revealed*. Seattle: Kenyon's Gospel, 1942.
———. *The Two Kinds of Knowledge*. Kenyon's Gospel, 1942.
———. *The Two Kinds of Life*. Kenyon's Gospel, 2002.
———. *The Two Kinds of Righteousness*. Kenyon's Gospel, 1965.
———. *What Happened from the Cross to the Throne*. Seattle: Kenyon's Gospel, 1969.
———. *The Wonderful Name of Jesus*. Kenyon's Gospel, n.d.
King, P. *Only Believe: Examining the Origin and Development of Classic and Contemporary Word of Faith Theologies*. Tulsa: Word and Spirit, 2008.
Kraft, C. *Christianity with Power: Your Worldview and Your Experience of the Supernatural*. Ann Arbor: Servant, 1989.
Kraft, C. "Spiritual Warfare: A Neocharismatic Perspective." In *New International Dictionary of Pentecostal and Charismatic Movements*, edited by S. Burgess et al., 1091–96. Grand Rapids: Zondervan, 2001.
Kwebena Asamoah-gyadu, J. "Pulling Down Strongholds: Evangelism, Principalities and Powers and the African Pentecostal Imagination." *International Review of Mission* 96 (2007) 306–17.
Ladd, G. E. "Kingdom of Christ, God, Heaven." In *The Evangelical Dictionary of Theology*, edited by W. Elwell, 607–11. Grand Rapids: Baker, 1986.
———. *The Presence of the Future*. Grand Rapids: Eerdmans, 1974.

Bibliography

Lampman, J. "Targeting Cities with 'Spiritual Mapping' Prayer." *Christian Science Monitor* (Sep 23, 1999) Online: http://www.csmonitor.com/1999/0923/p15s1.html.

Law, T. *Principles of Praise*. Tulsa: Victory, 1985.

Lawson, S. "Defeating Territorial Spirits." In *Territorial Spirits: Practical Strategies for How to Crush the Enemy Through Spiritual Warfare*, edited by C. P. Wagner, 55–66. Shippensburg, PA: Destiny Image, 2012.

Lewis, C. S. *The Screwtape Letters*. London: Geoffrey Bles, 1942.

Lie, G. "E. W. Kenyon: Cult Founder or Evangelical Minister?" *Journal of the European Pentecostal Theological Association* 16.1 (1996) 71–86.

———. "E. W. Kenyon: Cult Founder or Evangelical Minister?" MA diss., Lutheran School of Theology, 1998.

Lim, H. L. "Methodologies of Musicking in Practical Theology: A Portal into the World of Contemporary Worship Song." *International Journal of Practical Theology* 18.2 (2014) 305–16.

Lorenzo, V. "Evangelizing a City Dedicated to Darkness." In *Breaking Strongholds in Your City: How to Use Spiritual Mapping to Make Your Prayers More Strategic, Effective and Targeted*, edited by C. P. Wagner, 171–93. Ventura, CA: Regal, 1993.

Lossky, V. *The Mystical Theology of the Eastern Church*. Cambridge: James Clarke, 1991.

Lowe, C. *Territorial Spirits and World Evangelization: A Biblical, Historical, and Missiological Critique of Strategic-Level Spiritual Warfare*. Fearn: Christian Focus, 1998.

MacArthur Jr., J. *Charismatic Chaos*. Grand Rapids: Zondervan, 1992.

———. *Strange Fire: The Danger of Offending the Holy Spirit with Counterfeit Worship*. Nashville, TN: Thomas Nelson, 2013.

Magdelene. "Principalities-Powers-Rulers of Darkness-Wickedness." Online: http://www.battleinchrist.com/principalities_powers_world_rulers_of_darkness_spiritual_wickedness_in_spiritual_warfare.htm.

Maier, B., and P. Monroe. "A Theological Analysis of Theophostic Ministry." *Trinity Journal* 24 (2003) 169–88.

Maroney, E. *Religious Syncretism*. London: SCM, 2006.

Maudlin, M. G. "Seers in the Heartland: Hot on the Trail of the Kansas City Prophets." *Christianity Today* 35.1 (14 Jan 1991) 18–22.

Mayhue, Richard. "For What did Christ Atone in Isa 53:4–5?" *The Masters Seminary Journal* (Fall 1995) 121–41.

McConnell, D. *A Different Gospel*. London: Hodder and Stoughton, 1988.

McCrossan, T. J. *Bodily Healing and the Atonement*. Edited by R. Hicks and K. E. Hagin. Tulsa, OK: Kenneth Hagin Ministries, 1982.

McDermott, B. *Word Become Flesh: Dimensions of Christology*. Collegeville, MN.: Liturgical, 1993.

McDonnell, K. "Seven Documents on the Discipleship Question." In *Presence, Power, Praise: Documents on the Charismatic Renewal Vol. 2*, edited by K. McDonnell, 116–47. Collegeville, MN: Liturgical, 1980.

McFadden, M. "The Ironies of Pentecost: Phoebe Palmer, World Evangelism, and Female Networks." *Methodist History* 31.2 (Jan 1993) 133–57.

McGonigle, Herbert. "Pneumatological Nomenclature in Early Methodism." *Wesleyan Theological Journal* 8 (1973) 61–71.

McIntyre, J. *E. W. Kenyon and His Message of Faith: The True Story*. Lake Mary: Creation, 1997.

Bibliography

McLaren, Brian. *A New Kind of Christian*. San Francisco: Jossey Bass, 2001.
McNair Scot, B. *Apostles Today: Making Sense of Contemporary Charismatic Apostolates: A Historical and Theological Appraisal*. Eugene: Pickwick, 2014.
Menzies, R. "A Pentecostal Perspective on 'Signs and Wonders.'" *Pneuma* 17.2 (1993) 265–78.
Menzies, Robert. "Healing in the Atonement." In *Spirit and Power: Foundations of Pentecostal Experience*, edited by Robert and William Menzies, 160–68. Grand Rapids: Zondervan, 2000.
Menzies, W. W. *Anointed to Serve: The Story of the Assemblies of God*. Springfield: Gospel Publishing, 1971.
Meyer, J. *Battlefield of the Mind*. New York: Warner, 1995.
———. *Managing Your Emotions Instead of Your Emotions Managing You*. New York: Warner, 1998.
———. *Me and My Big Mouth: Your Answer is Right Under Your Nose*. New York: Warner, 2002.
———. "Mind, Mouth, Moods, and Attitudes." Personal Blog. Online: http://www.joycemeyer.org/ProductDetail.aspx?id=000592.
———. *The Secret Power of Speaking God's Word*. New York: Warner Faith, 2004.
———. *The Word, The Name, The Blood*. New York: Warner, 1995.
———. "Your Mouth is a Weapon." *Life in the Word* (March 1997) 2–4.
Milbank, J. *Theology and Social Theory: Beyond Secular Reason*. Revised Edition. Oxford: Blackwell, 2006.
———. *The Word Made Strange: Theology, Language, Culture*. Oxford: Blackwell, 1997.
Milbank, J., C. Pickstock, and G. Ward. *Radical Orthodoxy: A New Theology*. London: Routledge, 1999.
Miller, E. "The Bondage Maker: Examining the Message and Method of Neil T. Anderson, Part One: Sanctification and the Believer's Identity in Christ." *Christian Research Journal* 21.1 (1998).
Miller, E. "An Evaluation of Theophostic Prayer Ministry." *Christian Research Institute Position Paper* PST001 (2005) Online: http://theophostic.com/resources/1/pdf/PST001.pdf.
Missildine, H. *Your Inner Child of the Past*. New York: Simon and Schuster, 1963.
Mitchem, S. *Name it and Claim it: Prosperity Preaching in the Black Church*. Cleveland, OH: Pilgrim Press, 2007.
Monk, W. H., ed. *Hymns Ancient and Modern*. London: William Clowes, 1861.
Montgomery, Carrie Judd. *The Prayer of Faith*. London: Victory, 1930.
Moo, D. "Divine Healing in the Health and Wealth Gospel." *Trinity Journal* 9 (1988) 191–209.
Moody, G., and E. Moody. *Deliverance Manual*. Online: http://www.demonbuster.com/demonich.html.
Moore, S. D. *The Shepherding Movement*. Edinburgh: T. & T. Clark, 2003.
Moriarty, M. G. *The New Charismatics*. Grand Rapids: Zondervan, 1992, 77.
Murphy, E. *A Handbook for Spiritual Warfare*. Nashville, TN: Thomas Nelson. 1992.
Murray, Stuart. *Post-Christendom: Church and Mission in a Strange New World*. Milton Keynes: Paternoster, 2004.
Nee, W. *Spiritual Authority*. New York: Christian Fellowship, 2014.
Neuman, H. T. "Cultic Origins of the Word-Faith Theology Within the Charismatic Movement." *Pneuma* 12.1 (1990) 32–55.

Bibliography

Newton, J. "Pentecostalism in Australia: Where's it at and Where's it Going?" European Pentecostal Theological Association Annual Conference, Florence. 1 July 2015.

Nichol, J. T. *Pentecostalism: The Story of the Growth and Development of a Vital New Force in American Protestantism.* New York: Harper & Row, 1966.

Niehaus, J. "Old Testament Foundations: Signs and Wonders in Prophetic Ministry and the Substitutionary Atonement of Is.53." In *The Kingdom and the Power*, edited by G. S. Greig and K. Springer, 48–50. Ventura, CA: Regal, 1995.

Nyanni, C. "Spirit Baptism and Power: Luke's Concept of Spirit and Power Reflected in the Church of Pentecost with Specific Reference to the Church of Pentecost in Birmingham, England." MPhil diss., University of Manchester, 2014.

Oliver, M. *History of Philosophy.* London: Hamlyn, 2000.

Ortiz, J. *Disciple.* London: Marshall, Morgan & Scott, 1975.

Otis Jr., G. "An Overview of Spiritual Mapping." In *Breaking Strongholds in Your City.* Edited by C.P. Wagner, 29–47. Tunbridge Wells: Monarch, 1993.

———. *The Twilight Labyrinth: Why Does Spiritual Darkness Linger Where It Does?* Grand Rapids: Chosen, 1997.

———. *Transformations: A Documentary.* London: Sentinel Ministries UK, 1999.

———. *Transformations II: The Glory Spreads.* London: Sentinel Ministries UK, 2001.

Packer, J. I., et al., *The Kingdom and the Power: Are Healing and the Spiritual Gifts Used by Jesus and the Early Church Meant for the Church Today?: A Biblical Look at How to Bring the Gospel to the World with Power.* Ventura, CA: Regal, 1993.

Page, N. *And Now let's Move into a Time of Nonsense: Why Worship Songs are Failing the Church.* Milton Keynes: Authentic, 2004.

Page, S. H. T. *Powers of Evil: A Biblical Study of Satan and Demons.* Leicester: Apollos, 1995.

Palmer, P. *Faith and its Effects, or, Fragments from my Portfolio.* London: Alexander Heylin, 1856.

Patterson, B. "Cause for Concern." *Christianity Today* (Aug 8, 1986) 20.

Penn-Lewis, J. *Life in the Spirit.* Fort Washington: Christian Literature Crusade, 1991.

Percy, M. "Sweet Rapture: Subliminal Eroticism in Contemporary Charismatic Worship." *Theology and Sexuality* 6 (1997) 71–106.

———. *Words, Wonders and Power: Understanding Contemporary Christian Fundamentalism and Revivalism.* London: SPCK, 1996.

Peretti, F. *This Present Darkness.* New York: Howard, 1986.

Perriman, A. *Faith, Health and Prosperity.* Carlisle: Paternoster, 2003.

Petts, David. "Healing & the Atonement." PhD diss., University of Nottingham, 1993.

Polman, G, "The Pentecostal Conference in Germany." *Confidence* 2.2 (Feb. 1909) 33.

Powell, G., and S. *Christian Set Yourself Free.* Chichester: New Wine, 1983.

Pratt, T. "The Need for Dialogue: A Review of the Debate on the Controversy of Signs, Wonders, Miracles and Spiritual Warfare Raised in the Literature of the Third Wave Movement," *Pneuma* 13.1 (1991) 7–32.

Price, C. "The Wonder of Wimber." *Christianity* (Jan 1998) 7.

Prince, D. *Atonement: Your Appointment with God.* Baldock: Derek Prince Ministries UK, 2000.

———. *Blessing or Curse: You can Choose!* Milton Keynes: Word, 1990.

———. *The Divine Exchange: The Sacrificial Death of Jesus Christ on the Cross.* Harpenden: Derek Prince Ministries UK, 1995.

BIBLIOGRAPHY

———. "Kensington Temple Sep 1992. The Cross in My Life." *Keys to Successful Living*. Audiotape. Enfield: Derek Prince Ministries UK, 1992.

———. "Redemption: Plan and Fulfilment. The Exchange at the Cross." *Keys to Successful Living*. Audiotape. Fort Lauderdale: Derek Prince Ministries International, 1989.

Pugh, B. *Atonement Theories: A Way Through the Maze*. Eugene, OR: Cascade, 2014.

———. "Power in the Blood: The Significance of the Blood of Jesus to the Spirituality of Early British Pentecostalism and its Precursors." PhD diss., Bangor University, 2009.

———. *The Old Rugged Cross: A History of the Atonement in Popular Christian Devotion*. Eugene, OR: Cascade, 2016.

Pulkingham, B., and J. Harper, eds. *Sound of Living Waters: Songs of the Renewal*. London: Hodder & Stoughton, 1974.

———. *Fresh Sounds*. London: Hodder & Stoughton, 1976.

Pytches, D. *Does God Speak Today?* London: Hodder and Stoughton, 1989.

———. *Some Said it Thundered*. London: Hodder and Stoughton, 1990.

Randall, I. M. "'Days of Pentecostal Overflowing': Baptists and the Shaping of Pentecostalism." In *The Gospel in the World: Studies in Baptist History and Thought, Vol.1*, edited by David Bebbington, 80–104. Carlisle: Paternoster, 2002.

———. "Old Time Power: Relationships between Pentecostalism and Evangelical Spirituality in England." Pneuma 19.1 (Spring 1997) 53–80.

Redman, M., *Jesus Christ (Once Again)*. Eastbourne: Kingsway, 1995.

———. *The Unquenchable Worshipper*. Eastbourne: Kingsway, 2001.

———. "Revelation and Response." In *The Heart of Worship Files*. Edited by M. Redman, 11–14. Eastbourne: Kingsway, 2003.

Reichenbach, Bruce. "By His Stripes We Are Healed." *Journal of the Evangelical Theological Society* 41.4 (Dec 1998) 551–60.

Robeck, C., and A. Yong, "Global Pentecostalism: An Introduction to an Introduction." In *A Cambridge Companion to Pentecostalism*, edited by C. Robeck and A. Yong, 1–10. New York: Cambridge University Press, 2014.

Robertson, E. "An Evaluative History of Covenant Ministries International and its Offshoots from 1995 to the Present Day." *Journal of the European Pentecostal Theological Association* 26.2 (2007) 75–91.

Robinson, J. *Divine Healing: The Formative Years: 1830–1890*. Eugene: Pickwick, 2011.

———. *Divine Healing: The Pentecostal-Holiness Transition Years: 1890–1906*. Eugene: Pickwick, 2013.

———. *Divine Healing: The Years of Expansion, 1906–1930, Theological Variation in the Transatlantic World*. Eugene: Pickwick, 2014.

Rooms, N. "'Nice Process, Shame about the Content': The *Alpha* Course in Three Different Cultural Contexts." *JATE* 2.2 (2005) 129–44.

Rose, G., P. Hughes, and G. D. Bouma. *Re-Imagining Church: Positive Ministry Responses to the Age of Experience*. Melbourne: Christian Research Association, 2014.

Sanford, A. *Sealed Orders*. Plainfield, NJ: Logos, 1972.

———. *The Healing Gifts of the Spirit*. New York: Pillar, 1966.

———. *The Healing Light*. New York: Balantine, 1983.

Sarles, K. "An Appraisal of the Signs and Wonders Movement." *Bibliotheca Sacra* 145 (1988) 57–82.

———. "A Theological Evaluation of the Prosperity Gospel." *Bibliotheca Sacra* 143.152 (1986) 329–52.

Schrieter, R. *Constructing Local Theologies*. London: SCM, 1985.

Bibliography

Scotland, N. "From the 'Not Yet' to the 'Now and Not Yet': Charismatic Kingdom Theology 1960–2010." *Journal of Pentecostal Theology* 20 (2011) 272–90.

———. *Charismatics and the Next Millennium: Do They Have a Future?* London: Hodder & Stoughton, 1995.

Scott Moreau, A. "Gaining Perspective on Territorial Spirits." Online: http://www.lausanne.org/content/territorial-spirits#N_50_.

Seamands, D. *Healing of Memories.* Amersham-on-the-Hill: Scripture, 1985.

Seet, C. "The Doctrine of Healing in the Atonement." *The Burning Bush* 2.2 (1996) 93–99.

Shakarian, D., J. Sherrill, and E. Sherrill. *The Happiest People on Earth.* London: Hodder & Stoughton, 1975.

Shelhamer, E. E., ed. *Finney on Revival.* Minneapolis: Bethany, n.d.

Shepherd, D. H. *A Critical Analysis of Power Evangelism as an Evangelistic Methodology of the Signs and Wonders Movement.* Mid-America Baptist Theological Seminary, 1991.

Sherrill, J. *They Speak with Other Tongues.* London: Hodder & Stoughton, 1964.

Shuttleworth, A. "A Critical Discussion of the Theology of Bill Johnson." *Journal of the European Pentecostal Theological Association* 35.2 (October 2015) 101–14.

Simpson, A. B. *Standing on Faith.* London: Marshall, Morgan & Scott, n.d.

Simpson, C. *The Challenge to Care.* Ann Arbor: Vine, 1986.

Sjöberg, K. "Spiritual Mapping for Prophetic Prayer Actions." In *Breaking Strongholds in Your City,* edited by C. P. Wagner, 97–119. Tunbridge Wells: Monarch, 1993.

Smail, T. "The Cross and the Spirit: Towards a Theology of Renewal." In *Charismatic Renewal: The Search for a Theology,* edited by Thomas Smail, Andrew Walker and Nigel Wright, 49–70. London: SPCK, 1995.

Smail, T., A. Walker, and N. Wright, "'Revelation Knowledge' and Knowledge of Revelation: The Faith Movement and the Question of Heresy." In *Charismatic Renewal: The Search for a Theology,* edited by T. Smail, A. Walker, and N. Wright, 133–51. London: SPCK, 1995.

Smith, E. *Beyond Tolerable Recovery: Moving Beyond Tolerable Existence into Genuine Restoration and Emotional Inner Healing.* Campbellsville, KY: Family Care, 1996.

———. *Healing Life's Hurts: Experiencing the Peace of Christ through Theophostic Prayer.* Campbellsville, KY: New Creation, 2005.

———. "History of TPM." Online: http://www.transformationprayer.org/history-of-transformation-prayer-ministry-previously-known-as-theophostic-prayer/.

Smith, G. R. "The Church Militant: A Study of 'Spiritual Warfare' in the Anglican Charismatic Renewal." PhD diss., University of Birmingham, 2011.

Smith, J. C. "Signs of the Times." In *Pentecostal Doctrine,* edited by Percy Brewster, 381–90. Percy Brewster, 1976.

Smith, J. K. A. *Introducing Radical Orthodoxy.* Grand Rapids: Baker, 2004.

———. "What Hath Cambridge to do with Azusa Street? Radical Orthodoxy and Pentecostal Theology in Conversation." *Pneuma* 25.1 (Spring 2003) 97–114.

Songs and Hymns of Fellowship. Eastbourne: Kingsway, 1991.

Songs of Fellowship Volume 1. Eastbourne: Kingsway, 1981.

Stead, G., and M. Stead. *The Exotic Plant: A History of the Moravian Church in Great Britain 1742–2000.* Peterborough: Epworth, 2003.

Stearns, R. "Why Israel Matters." *Charisma* 31.10. *Charisma Magazine,* May 2006. Online: http://www.charismamag.com/blogs/146-j15/covers/cover-story/1912-why-israel-matters.

Bibliography

Steiner, K. "War and Peace Theology in German and Swedish Christin Zionism." *International Dialogue: a Multidisciplinary Journal of World Affairs* 3 (2013) 38–76.

Steven, J. "Charismatic Hymnody in the Light of Early Methodist Hymnody." *Studia Liturgica* 27.2 (1997) 217–34.

Stevens, D. "Daniel 10 and the Notion of Territorial Spirits." *Bibliotheca Sacra* 157 (Oct-Dec 2000) 410–31.

Subritzky, B. *Demons Defeated*. Tonbridge: Sovereign World, 1985.

Synan, V. *The Century of the Holy Spirit*. Nashville, TN: Thomas Nelson, 2001.

———. "Frank Bartleman and Azusa Street." In *Azusa Street: the Roots of Modern-day Pentecost*, edited by Frank Bartleman, ix–xxv. Plainfield: Bridge, 1980.

———. "A Healer in the House? A Historical Perspective on Healing in the Pentecostal/Charismatic Tradition." *Asian Journal of Pentecostal Studies* 3.2 (2000) 189–201.

———. *The Pentecostal-Holiness Tradition: Charismatic Movements in the Twentieth Century*. Grand Rapids: Eerdmans, 1997.

Tharp, D. T. *Signs and Wonders in the Twentieth Century Evangelical Church: Corinth Revisited*. Ashland, OH: Ashland Theological Seminary, 1992.

Tomlinson, D. "Shepherding: Care or Control?" In *Harmful Religion: An Exploration of Religious Abuse*, edited by L. Osborn and A. Walker, 26–42. London: SPCK, 1997.

Trine, R. W. *In Tune with the Infinite*. New Canaan: Keats, 1973.

Trudinger, R. *Master Plan: God's Foundation Stones for Church Restoration*. Basingstoke: Olive Tree, 1980.

Unger, M. "Divine Healing." *Biblotheca Sacra* 128.511 (July 1971) 234–44.

Van der Meer, E. "Strategic Level Spiritual Warfare and Mission in Africa." *Evangelical Review of Mission* 34 (2010) 155–66.

Vaughan Williams, R. *National Music*. London: Oxford University Press, 1963.

Velthuysen, D. "A Pastoral Theological Examination of Inner Healing." PhD diss., Rhodes University, 1989.

Virgo, T. *Enjoying God's Grace*. Milton Keynes: Word, 1989.

———. *God's Lavish Grace*. Oxford: Monarch, 2004.

———. *No Well-Worn Paths*. Eastbourne: Kingsway, 2001.

Vondey, W. *Pentecostalism: A Guide for the Perplexed*. London: Bloomsbury, 2013.

Wagner, C. P. *Confronting the Powers*. Ventura, CA: Regal, 1996.

———. *Engaging the Enemy*. Grand Rapids: Baker, 1991.

———. *Prayer Shield*. Ventura: Regal Books, 1992.

———. *Praying With Power*. Grand Rapids: Baker, 1997.

———. "Territorial Spirits." In *Wrestling with Dark Angels*. Edited by C.P. Wagner and D. Pennoyer. 83–102. Ventura, CA: Regal Books, 1990.

———. "Territorial Spirits and World Missions." *Evangelical Missions Quarterly* 25:3 (July 1989) 278–288.

———. *The Third Wave of the Holy Spirit: Encountering the Power of Signs and Wonders Today*. Ann Arbor: Servant Publications Vine, 1988.

———. *Warfare Prayer: What the Bible Says About Spiritual Warfare*. Ventura, CA: Regal, 1992.

Waldvogel, E. "The 'Overcoming' Life: A Study in the Reformed Evangelical Contribution to Pentecostalism." *Pneuma* 1.1 (1979) 7–17.

Walker, A. "The Devil You Think You Know: Demonology and the Charismatic Movement." In *Charismatic Renewal*, edited by T. Smail, A.Walker, and N. Wright, 86–105. London: SPCK, 1995.

———. *Enemy Territory: The Christian Struggle for the World.* London: Hodder & Stoughton, 1987.

———. *Restoring the Kingdom: The Radical Christianity of the House Church Movement.* Guildford: Eagle, 1998.

Walker, D. *Catching the Initiatives of Heaven: The Key to Accessing the Power if Heaven for Every Need on Earth.* Las Vegas, NV: Dunamis Resources, 2010.

Ward, G. *True Religion.* Oxford: Blackwell, 2003.

Ward, P. "Alpha—the McDonaldization of Religion?" *Anvil* 15.4 (1998) 279–86.

———. *Growing Up Evangelical.* London: SPCK, 1996.

———. *Selling Worship.* Milton Keynes: Authentic, 2005.

Warnock, George. *The Feast of Tabernacles.* Springfield, MO: Bill Britton, 1951.

Warren, E.J. "'Spiritual Warfare': A Dead Metaphor?" *Journal of Pentecostal Theology* 21 (2012) 278–97.

Warrington, K. *Pentecostal Theology.* London: T. & T. Clark, 2008.

Watkins, K. "Congregational Song for Folk-Protestant Worship," *Worship* 46.2 (1972) 86–97.

Way of the Cross: The New Wine and Soul Survivor Song Book. Chorleywood: New Wine, 1996.

Weber, M. *The Theory of Social and Economc Organization.* Translated by A. M. Henderson and T. Parsons. Glencoe, IL: The Free Press, 1947.

Wessels, R. "The Sprit Baptism: Nineteenth Century Roots." *Pneuma* 14.2 (Fall 1992) 127–57.

Westerholm, S. *Perspectives Old and New on Paul: The "Lutheran" Paul and His Critics.* Grand Rapids: Eerdmans, 2004.

Whittaker, C. *Great Revivals.* Eastbourne: Victor, 2005.

Wilkinson, J. "Physical Healing and the Atonement." *Evangelical Quarterly* 63.2 (1991) 149–67.

Williams, D. "Charismatic Worship." In *Exploring the Worship Spectrum: Six Views,* edited by P. Engle and P. Basden, 137–72. Grand Rapids: Zondervan, 2004.

———. *Signs, Wonders, and the Kingdom of God: A Biblical Guide for the Reluctant Skeptic.* Ann Arbor: Vine, 1989.

Williams, D. T. "The Heresy of Prosperity Teaching: A Message for the Church in its Approach to Need." *Journal of Theology for Southern Africa* 61 (Dec 1987) 33–44.

———. "Prosperity Teaching and Positive Thinking," *Evangelical Review of Theology* 11.3 (July 1987) 197–208.

Williams, J. "The Pentecostalization of Christian Zionism." *Church History* 84.1 (March 2015) 159–94.

———. *Spirit Cure: A History of Pentecostal Healing.* Oxford: Oxford University Press, 2013.

Wimber J., and K. Springer. *Power Evangelism.* London: Hodder & Stoughton, 1985.

Wimber, J. "Power Evangelism Definitions and Directions." In *Supernatural Forces in Spiritual Warfare: Wrestling with Dark Angels,* edited by C.P. Wagner, 19–49. Shippensburg, PA: Destiny Image, 2012.

———. *Signs and Wonders and Church Growth.* Placentia, CA: Vineyard Ministries International, 1984.

———. "Worship: Intimacy with God." *Equipping the Saints* 1.1 (Jan/Feb 1987) 5.

Wimber, J., and K. Springer. *Power Encounters.* San Francisco: Harper & Row, 1988.

———. *Power Evangelism.* San Francisco: Harper & Row, 1986.

Bibliography

———. *Power Healing*. London: Hodder & Stoughton, 1986.

———. *Power Points*. San Francisco: Harper & Row, 1991.

Wink, W. *Naming the Powers: The Language of Power in the New Testament*. Philadelphia: Fortress, 1984.

Wood, H., *New Thought Simplified: How to Gain Harmony and Health*. Boston: Lothrop, Lee and Shepard, 1903.

Wright, C. "Lausanne Theology Working Group Statement on the Prosperity Gospel." *Evangelical Review of Theology* 34.2 (2010) 99–102.

Wright, N. "Deliverance and Exorcism in Theological Perspective: Is there Any Substance to Evil?" In *Exorcism and Deliverance: Multi-Disciplinary Studies*, edited by W. Kay and R. Parry, 203–21. Milton Keynes: Paternoster, 2011.

———. *The Fair Face of Evil*. London: Marshall Pickering 1989.

Yapko, M. *Suggestions of Abuse: True and False Memories of Childhood Sexual Trauma*. New York: Simon & Schuster, 1994.

Index

Alpha, 43, 106–7
Anderson, Neil, see Freedom in Christ
Apostolic Networks, xi, 21, 42, 58, 62
Assemblies of God, xi, 6, 16, 118
atonement, 28, 51–55, 78, 100, 124
Azusa Street, 2, 5–6

Baker, Heidi, 109, 118
baptism in the Holy Spirit, 1, 2–7, 12, 18–20, 40, 111
Bennett, Dennis, 18–20, 24, 61
Bethel Church, xiii, 90, 108, 118–19
Bethel Sozo, 25, 29–32
blood of Jesus, 6, 52–53
Boddy, Alexander, 3, 6, 8, 18
Bonnke, Reinhard, 106

Capps, Charles, 67, 70, 77, 80–82, 84–85
Carter-Stapleton, Ruth, 24, 28, 35–36
Cavanaugh, William, xvi, 64–65
cell groups, 57–58
conversion, 1. 5, 8, 16, 51, 55, 111
Copeland, Kenneth, 67, 70, 77–82, 84–86

Darby, John Nelson, 7, 9
discipleship, xvi–vii, 57–59, 61–62, 65–66, 121, 123
Drane, John, xv, 125
Durham, William, 5

eroticism in worship, 43, 46–48, 115
exorcism, 89, 90, 96

Finney, Charles, 3, 75, 106
Fletcher, John, 2
Fort Lauderdale Five, see Shepherding
freedom in Christ, 25, 31, 32–34
Full Gospel Businessmen's Fellowship International, 61
Fuller Theological Seminary, 88, 91–92, 110–11, 114

gifts of the Spirit, ix, xi, 1, 5, 8, 16, 18, 20–22, 25, 27–29, 40, 50, 111–12, 114
Gumbell, Nicky, see Alpha

Hagee, John, 10–11
Hagin, Kenneth, 67–71, 76–81, 84
Healing Evangelists, 106
healing
    and Bill Johnson, 118–20
    and Wimber, 111, 117
    and Word of Faith, 68–69, 72, 74–76
    general, 124, 126
    gift of, 5, 8, 18
    in the atonement, 1, 12–15, 22
    inner, xii–xiii, 23–37, 120, 122
    on the streets and Treasure Hunting, 108–9, 125
    revival, post WWII, 10, 88
Hiebert, Paul, 88, 90, 92, 102–3, 121
Hillsong, 44, 49
holiness movement, 1–3, 5–7, 12, 52–53, 74–75, 106

initial evidence, xiv, 1, 16–18

Index

Jesus Culture, 44, 108, 118
Jesus Movement, 39, 58
Johnson, Bill, 108–9, 118–20
Jones, Bryn, 40, 42, 60, 62–63

Kenyon, E.W., 68–71, 73–77, 79–81, 83–85
Keswick Convention, 3–4, 6–7, 17, 52

Ladd, George Eldon, 15, 97, 113, 119, 121

metaphysical cults, 25, 70, 74–75
Meyer, Joyce, 68, 81–84
Milbank, John, xv–xvii, 35, 125–26
modernity, xiv–xviii, 35, 54, 64–65, 109, 116–17, 123–25

Nee, Watchman, xiii, 60
New Thought, 25, 70–76, 83
New Wine, 43, 63

Ortiz, Juan Carlos, 59

Palmer, Phoebe, 2–3, 17, 76
Parham, Charles, 9, 17–18
Penn-Lewis, Jessie, 4, 87–88
Pentecostalism, Classical, xi–xiv, 1–23, 52, 106, 123
Percy, Martyn, 46–48, 115–17
perfectionism, see Holiness movement
Pickstock, Catherine, xvi, 35, 54, 105, 125
postmodern, postmodernity, xv–xvii, 48, 62, 83, 85, 100, 125
Power Encounters, 110, 112–14, 116, 119
premillennialism, 1, 7–12
Prince, Derek, 10, 14–15, 52, 56, 61, 88, 90
prophecy, 7, 10–11, 14, 17, 20–22, 112
prophet, office of, xvii, 20–22, 42, 58
Radical Orthodoxy, xv–xvi, 35, 64, 123, 125

Renewal, Charismatic, xi, xiii, 6, 10, 17–18, 24, 40–41, 61–62, 70, 90, 106, 111, 117, 123
Restoration, xvii, 8, 40–45, 58, 63
Revival Alliance, 109, 118, 121

Sanford, Agnes, 24–29, 35
secular, secularism, xiv–xviii, 35, 54, 61, 64–65, 86, 109, 112, 116–17, 121–22, 124–26
Seymour, William J., 18
Shakarian, Demos, 61, 106
shepherding, xii, xvii, 56–67, 116, 121–22
Signs and Wonders, xii, xvii, 12, 43, 90–91, 107–22
SLSW, see Spiritual Warfare
Smith, James, K. A., xvi–xviii, 35, 64, 125
Soul Survivor, 43–44, 53, 63
spiritual mapping, see spiritual warfare
spiritual warfare, xii, 53, 87–105, 116, 121–22

territorial spirits, see spiritual warfare
Theophostic Prayer Ministry, 25, 29–32
tongues, gift of, xiv, 1, 5–8, 14, 16–20, 24, 112
treasure hunting, 108–9

Vineyard, 42–43, 46–47, 109–11, 115, 117–18
Virgo, Terry, 42–43, 63, 124

Wagner, C. Peter, 89–92, 94–95, 99, 101–2, 110–11, 114, 118
Welsh Revival, 2, 4–5, 8
Wesley, John, 2–3, 5
Wimber, John, 15, 43, 89, 91, 97, 102, 110–22
Word of Faith, xii, 10, 25, 55, 67–86, 88, 116, 121–22, 124
worship, Charismatic, 10–11, 22, 38–55, 108, 115

Zionism, Christian, 9–11

www.ingramcontent.com/pod-product-compliance
Lightning Source LLC
Chambersburg PA
CBHW071506150426
43191CB00009B/1431